# HERNE HILL PERSONALITIES

Researched, written and produced by
George Young, Jeffrey Doorn, John Brunton,
Brenda Jones and Caroline Knapp.

## Biographies of 146 people who lived in Herne Hill

First published in 2006 for
The Herne Hill Society
PO Box 27845
LONDON SE24 9XA
by
Local History Publications
316 Green Lane
Streatham
London SW16 3AS



ISBN 1873520 60 3

# INTRODUCTION

The personality of an area is largely formed by the personalities who have lived there. Naturally, geography and location are also very important; indeed they are major factors in attracting people to an area. Herne Hill has been home to a wide variety of personalities, some famous, some infamous, some well known and celebrated only in their particular field.

When we gathered names for possible inclusion in this book, we found ourselves with some 320 - far too many! We thus established guidelines, eliminating those who visited or contributed to Herne Hill but never lived here. It also seemed unfair, if not intrusive, to include those still alive, whether currently resident or moved on. We could thus concentrate on people now dead who lived here and whose character, life-circumstances or achievements are of lasting and far-reaching significance.

We may have bent the rules occasionally, e.g. for noteworthy individuals held in deep local affection, or people who lived on the outer fringes of the area but were intimately connected with Herne Hill and its other personalities. Equally, we had to exclude certain names, either at the request of their surviving family or because we could find no conclusive proof they lived here.

The resulting biographies all chronicle true personalities with interesting qualities that make for individuality and real character. Many are connected, either as family, friends, business associates or partners. We know for instance that John Ruskin received and visited artists and collectors in the area, like the Bicknells across the street. One can speculate whether he socialised with Henry Bessemer, his next-door neighbour in the 1860s. It has been said that Bransby Williams commissioned monologues, e.g. 'The Pigtail of Li Fan Fu' from Sax Rohmer. With all their theatrical connections, did the Rohmers welcome the Lupinos into the neighbourhood? Did Ida Lupino and Roddy McDowall meet in Hollywood and discuss their Herne Hill childhoods? There is a link between Charles Woolley and William Strudwick; but did Woolley ever meet fellow journalist H D Lowry, seven doors along Dulwich Road? Did liberated young artist Rotimi Fani-Kayode visit elder liberationist C L R James, seven doors down Railton Road? The possibilities for imaginary conversations are endless!

A word about addresses, some of which changed many times over the years: headings show street numbers as they were at the time of residence or, for Denmark Hill and Herne Hill, at the 1883 numbering. The text indicates where houses have since been renumbered. For houses now gone, their location is given.

In today's celebrity obsessed world, any Big Brother contestant or one-hit boyband member is accorded instant fame. Surely personality is deeper and longer lasting than mere celebrity. Thus, from the eminence that is Herne Hill, we celebrate our eminent former residents, as well as those neither famous nor admired, whose lives deserve recognition and whose stories demand retelling.

The arts, science, medicine, business, commerce, law, politics, religion, sports: all life is here. We honour the great and the good, shake our heads at the unfortunate and the evil. In one way or another, they have all left their mark.

# ACKNOWLEDGEMENTS

Our grateful thanks go to the following for their help, advice and information:

Ellen Barbett, Bishopsgate Library, Brian Bloice, John Brown, Lady Judith Buckley, Mrs Leela Carter, Alan Curtis, Jill Dudman, George Vaughan Ellis, Ann Faning, Bob Flanagan, Annie Gelly, Dave Gelly, Paul Graham, Robert Holden, Institution of Civil Engineers, Patricia Jenkyns, Michael Kilgarriff, Lambeth Archives, Valerie Browne Lester, Linnean Society of London, Mrs Lysbeth Merrifield, London Metropolitan Archives, Lord Thomson of Monifeith, National Trust, Patrick Newley, John Pile, Geoffrey Powell, Alan Sanders, John Smallwood, Southwark Local History Studies Library, Ron Spears, Lisa Voden-Decker, Michael Walker, Daphne Watts; and Damaris Dodds for the indexing.

For their kind permission to use illustrations: British Library, Chetham's Library (Manchester), Lucy Davies (198 Gallery), Ann Faning, Guildhall Library (City of London), Narinder Johal, The King's College Archives (King's College, London), Lambeth Landmark, Daphne Marchant, National Portrait Gallery (London), Bill Norton (Yeoman of the Queen's Body Guard), Ruskin Foundation (Ruskin Library, University of Lancaster), St John Ambulance, Dean and Chapter of Southwark Cathedral, the Southwark Art Collection, Southwark Local History Studies Library.

Published with the support of Heritage Lottery Awards for All

**Joe Randolph Ackerley (1896-1967)**
**4 Warmington Road**
**Writer and Editor**

Joe Randolph Ackerley was born 4 November 1896, the second of three children born to Alfred Roger Ackerley (1863-1929) and his mistress Janette Katherine Aylward (1864-1946), an actress. Alfred, a widower, declined to marry Janette for fear of losing a £2,000 a year allowance he received from his former in-laws. However, Alfred and Katherine did eventually marry in 1919. Joe was born at 4 Warmington Road, the home of his grandmother, where Alfred had placed Janette following the birth of their first son the previous year.

Joe served as an officer in the First World War, an experience that produced in him a profound melancholy. He first acknowledged his homosexuality while a prisoner of war in 1917; and the only close friendship in his life was with the writer EM Forster.

In 1921, after graduating in English from Cambridge University, Joe spent some years in India as companion/secretary to the eccentric Maharajah of Chatpur. During this time he published, in 1923, an anthology of poems. In 1925, a play, *Prisoners of War*, based on his WW1 experiences and exploring the themes of war and homosexuality, was produced in London.

In 1925 Joe became an Assistant Producer at the BBC. At the same time he was appointed Literary Editor of *The Listener*, a post he held until 1949. His book *Hindoo Holiday*, based on his Indian diaries, was published in 1932. In spite of problems of libel and obscenity, the book's humour and character depiction consolidated his reputation.

Both father and son were sexually unorthodox. As a handsome practising homosexual, Joe searched among working class men for the Ideal Friend. Alfred had two mistresses, leading a secret double life and supporting two households. It was only after his father's death that Joe discovered that Alfred had had a 'wife' and three daughters living in Cheshire.

In 1956 Joe published *My Dog Tulip*, a frank and funny portrait of his dog Queenie. His W H Smith Award-winning novel *We Think the World of You* (1960) was based on his love of a petty criminal, the dog's owner, and the transference of that love to the dog. Joe became an advocate for animal rights.

In 1968 Joe published *My Father and Myself*, a family memoir. In retirement he lived in Putney with Queenie, an aged aunt Bunny and his emotionally unstable sister Nancy. The dog's death in 1961 increased his melancholy; but he still wrote witty and self-deprecating letters.

Joe Ackerley died from a coronary thrombosis on 4 June 1967. He was cremated at Putney Vale crematorium.

## Joan Agnew (1846-1924)
## 28 Herne Hill
## Cousin of John Ruskin

Christened Joanna Ruskin Tweddale Sproat Agnew, she was born in Wigtown, Scotland, 4 March 1846, the eighth of nine children. The daughter of George Agnew, Hereditary Sheriff-Clerk of Wigtown, and Catherine Tweddale, Joan shared great-grandparents Rev. James Tweddale and Janet Adair with John Ruskin. She was thus his second cousin, later becoming his ward and then adopted by him; she is the relative most associated with Ruskin.

She first visited 163 Denmark Hill on 19 April 1864, soon after the death of John's father, John James Ruskin. John felt that his mother, then aged 82, needed companionship. Joan had come for just one week, but as the two women became instant friends she stayed for seven years until her marriage.

In his autobiography *Praeterita*, Ruskin wrote of Joan that he felt instinctively that "... the gift both to my mother and me was one which we should not easily bear to be again withdrawn." On her marriage to Arthur Severn in 1871, Ruskin's early home at 28 Herne Hill was given to Joan for the rest of the lease. The Severns later renewed the lease for a further 21 years, and used the house until 1907.

Joan and Arthur had five children, three sons and two daughters, and would visit Ruskin when he moved to Brantwood in the Lake District. When in Herne Hill, Joan received daily letters from him. Ruskin's letters to other people are full of references to "Joanna's care". He called her his "pet cousin" when writing an account of his material affairs; and her "... children, and their donkey need good supplies of bread and butter, and hay; she is always promising to keep my old nursery for a lodging for me, when I come to town."

Joan wrote in 1899 how she and Ruskin were "distressed by the way Herne Hill has completely changed its character and surroundings, the greater part of it now being built over by houses that spring up like mushrooms, covering the old grounds and gardens that were beautiful only a few years ago."

Joan tended her cousin with a daughter's care, especially during his declining years when she and her family moved to be with him at Brantwood. In 1885, Ruskin made over Brantwood to the Severns by deed of gift, with the stipulation that they must not sell the estate nor let any large portion be built on. This large home suited them, with the necessary space for their children and a studio added for Arthur. On Ruskin's death in 1900 Joan became one of his literary executors, and unveiled monuments to him in Westminster Abbey and on Friar's Crag, Keswick. Joan died at Brantwood on 26 June 1924, leaving £9,945 in her will.

## Charles Alcock (1842-1907)
## 319 Norwood Road
## Sports Journalist
## and Founder of the FA Cup

Charles William Alcock, born 2 December 1842, was the second of six sons of Charles Alcock, a wealthy ship owner and insurance broker of Sunderland, and his wife Elizabeth, née Forster. He was educated at Forest School, Walthamstow and at Harrow

(1855-59). With his elder brother, John Forster Alcock, he played football for the Forest Club and later he formed the Wanderers Club. His brother, as representative of the Forest Club, attended the momentous meeting of the Football Association (FA) in 1863 when it was agreed that a formal set of rules for football be adopted, and that handling the ball and deliberate kicking of opponents be stopped.

In 1866 Charles Alcock was elected to the F A committee, and was appointed its Honorary Secretary in 1870, a post he held until 1890. From 1890-96 he was the paid FA Secretary and in 1896 was appointed a vice-president.

In 1871 Alcock suggested that a competition be established, open to all footballing clubs, for the prestige of winning a trophy, the FA Challenge Cup. The rules were based on his experience of the knock-out house competitions he had known at Harrow School. The first cup final was held at the Oval when Alcock's own team, The Wanderers, beat The Royal Engineers by 1-0. Only 15 clubs took part in that first competition; but it stimulated other clubs to join the FA. By 1884, 100 clubs had taken part. Alcock refereed the finals of 1875 and 1879. From 1895-1914, the final was played at the grounds of the Crystal Palace, and from 1923 at Wembley.

In 1870 Alcock introduced the first international football match, when an unofficial game was played with a Scottish side at the Oval. Alcock captained England, who won 1-0. The first official international was in Glasgow (0-0 draw) in 1872, and led to the formation of the Scottish FA. The World Cup itself is an extension of his two inspired ideas.

Cricket was Alcock's other passion, having played for the Gentlemen of Essex.

In addition to his Football Association work he was also Secretary of Surrey County Cricket Club (SCCC), 1872-1907.

Surrey was very successful during this period, winning the championship eight times between 1872 and 1895. It was due to Alcock's cricket connection that the FA Cup Finals were played at the Oval.

In 1864 Alcock married Eliza Overden and the couple had two sons and six daughters. From c1873 to 1877 they lived at Jersey Lodge, the house formerly on the site of the present 319 Norwood Road, where one son and two daughters were born. The son, Charles Ernest, died in 1874 aged five months and was the first burial in the family plot at Norwood Cemetery. The parents, the other son and one daughter were later buried there. In 1999, a replacement headstone was erected in the Cemetery, funded by the FA, SCCC and the Friends of Norwood Cemetery.

Never settling in one house for more than a few years, the family's other addresses included West Dulwich, Brixton, Streatham, Richmond and Kew. Charles Alcock died on 26 February 1907 at Brighton.

## George Allen (1832-1907)
## The Lodge, 163 Denmark Hill
## Publisher and assistant to John Ruskin

George Allen was born 26 March 1832 at Newark-on-Trent, Nottinghamshire. In 1849 he was apprenticed as a carpenter to his uncle's building business in Clerkenwell and became a skilled joiner. He met John Ruskin in 1854 when he joined the landscape drawing class at the newly formed Working Men's College in Red Lion Square. A talented pupil, he became assistant drawing master at the college, working alongside Ruskin and Rossetti. On 25 December 1856 he married Anne Eliza 'Hannah' Hobbes, Ruskin's mother's maid. The couple had four sons and four daughters and came to live in the Lodge at the entrance to John Ruskin's house, 163 Denmark Hill.

In 1857 Ruskin made George his full-time assistant. Later, in 1871 and following a break-up with his former publishers, Ruskin helped George set up a company, George Allen, to publish his works. That same year, on the death of Ruskin's mother and sale of 163 Denmark Hill, George moved the family home to Orpington. From there he ran the business, storing his book stock in a garden shed. In 1890 he moved his offices to London, first to Chancery Lane, then to larger premises in Charing Cross Road. Although Ruskin's works remained the main business, George Allen also published biographies, travel books and reprinted fairy tales and standard literary works.

George died at his home in Orpington on 5 September 1907, and was buried in the parish churchyard. His wife had died eight months previously, in her eightieth year. The sons William and Hugh and daughter Grace carried on the business. However, the firm went bankrupt in 1913. A year later its assets were sold to Stanley Unwin, leading to the formation of a new company, George Allen and Unwin.

The Lodge, where George and his family lived from around 1861 to 1871, was demolished in 1947 along with the house itself, to make way for the present development of flats and houses.

## Charles George Ammon (1873-1960)
## 76 and 70 Ferndene Road
## Trade Unionist and Politician

Born 22 April 1873 into a poor Southwark household, Charles Ammon was the eldest of five children of Charles Ammon (d 1887), a cutler and toolmaker, and his wife Mary (1851-1900).

Aged eleven, Charles started work in a bottle factory. At 14 he joined the Post Office as a telegraph messenger and after five years was promoted to Sorter. He soon became actively involved with the Sorters' trade union; within two years was appointed Branch Secretary and to the Central Executive Committee. In 1893 he became a founder member of the Independent Labour Party.

Over the next two decades Charles became increasingly prominent in both the trade union movement and in the Labour Party. In 1920 he played a decisive role in establishing the Union of Post Office Workers, through merging the various unions representing individual groups of postal workers. In the same year he was elected the Union's Organising Secretary. At this time, Charles was also extending his interests into local and national politics. He was a member for North Camberwell of the London County Council 1919-25, and from 1922-31 was MP for the same Division. He was on the Labour Party National Executive from 1921-27, and from 1929-31 was Parliamentary Secretary to the Admiralty.

After losing elections in 1931, Charles regained his LCC seat in 1934. A year later he also regained his Parliamentary seat, which he held until 1944. In that year he became Baron Ammon of Camberwell, the first trade union peer. From 1945 he served as Government Chief Whip in the House of Lords and was appointed Chair of what was to become the National Dock Labour Board. However, in 1949 he was dismissed from both positions following a dispute with Prime Minister Atlee over an escalating dock strike.

Charles was Mayor of Camberwell in 1950-51 and frequently spoke in the Lords until he was disabled by a stroke in February 1955. He died in King's College Hospital 2 April 1960.

In 1898 Charles had married Ada Eileen May (d 1958). They had a son (d 1909), and two daughters, May and Ada. Charles moved with his family to live at 76 Ferndene Road c1931. Sometime around 1943 they moved to 70 Ferndene Road, where Charles lived until his death.

## Rev. Matthew Anderson (1799-1893) 2, 64 and 127 Herne Hill Vicar of St Paul's Church

Matthew Anderson was born in Ireland. He was ordained in 1824 and in the same year appointed Forces' Chaplain at Charlton-next-Woolwich. In 1827 he became Minister of the East Dulwich Chapel of Ease, remaining until 1844, when he resigned to become the first Vicar at the newly built church of St Paul's, Herne Hill.

In February 1858, the church was destroyed by fire; only the tower, spire and outer walls remained. Fortunately Matthew Anderson had had the foresight to insure the church building, from his own pocket, for £3,500. This enabled the church to be rebuilt at a cost of £5,200 - the balance being met from donations. The new church reopened 21 October 1858; it could accommodate 700 people and was rather more highly regarded than the old building. John Ruskin called it "one of the loveliest in the country and one that makes the fire a matter of rejoicing". The building is now Grade II* listed.

As Vicar of St Paul's, Matthew Anderson lived at a house on the site of 2 Herne Hill until the 1850s when he moved to 64 Herne Hill, almost opposite the church. This house was demolished in the 1880s; 172/174 Herne Hill now occupy the site. In 1867 he went to live in the newly built vicarage at 35 (now number 127) Herne Hill. There he stayed until 1869, when he was appointed Rector of Kemberton with Sutton Maddock, in Shropshire. In 1893 he moved to Seddlescombe Rectory in Battle, Sussex, but died there soon afterwards on 3 February that year.

## Benjamin Attwood (1794-1874)
## 169 Denmark Hill
## Philanthropist

In 1865, Benjamin Attwood inherited nearly £900,000 and Dulwich Hill House from his nephew, Matthias Wolverley Attwood. He was sole executor of the will and the main beneficiary. Already retired and financially comfortable, he tried to dispose of his fortune by donating sums of £1,000 to all manner of charities, as well as sums to his less prosperous kinsfolk. A benevolent institution, such as a hospital, would receive a visit from him. A cheque for £1,000 would be left, with a request that a simple acknowledgement in *The Times* be made and that his name never be disclosed. At his death, he left no will and his estate for administration was valued at nearly £600,000. According to the census records, he was unmarried.

Born in Halesowen, Shropshire, Benjamin was the youngest brother of Matthias Attwood and Thomas Attwood (1783-1856), bankers. His business life was in the manufacture of window glass, first in Birmingham and later at 25 New Bridge Street, Blackfriars. In the 1850s, he moved to 35 Grove End Road, St Johns Wood. After inheriting 169 Denmark Hill, he used it as a second home. In the late 1860s on leaving St Johns Wood, he moved to Pengelly House, Church Gate near the New River at Cheshunt, Hertfordshire where he died 22 November 1874. Benjamin is buried in Cheshunt Cemetery.

169 Denmark Hill, sometimes called Dulwich Hill House, was a large, detached mansion located midway between Sunray Avenue and Red Post Hill. Thomas Lynne Bristowe lived there c1875-88. The house was demolished c1890 and Sunray Avenue was laid out across the grounds in 1894. The gate-house serving the property, Hillcrest Lodge, was demolished c1961. It was located near the junction of Sunray Avenue and Denmark Hill, and also served the neighbouring Bessemer Estate.

## Matthias Attwood (1779-1851)
## 169 Denmark Hill
## MP and Banker

***Shield on Attwood tomb in Norwood Cemetery***

Born in Halesowen, Shropshire, Matthias was the second of seven sons of Matthias Attwood (1746-1836). Attwood senior had made a large fortune in Swedish iron, and with his gains founded a private bank, Attwoods (later Spooner & Attwoods) of 27 Gracechurch Street in the City of London.

On joining his father's firm, Matthias junior showed great banking ability and talent for dealing with the financial and political questions of the time. In the 1810s he distinguished himself by his opposition to the resumption of cash payments, writing two pamphlets on the subject and persuading William Cobbett (1763-1835), a champion of the poor, to his way of thinking. Even Robert Peel (1788-1850), the then chairman of the Bank Committee, was impressed by the strength of his arguments. (Note: As a wartime measure in 1797 the Bank of England suspended cash payments in exchange for its bank notes so it could supply the government with the large amounts of gold needed to pay for the Napoleonic war. Cash payments resumed in 1819 after much deliberation by the Bank Committee.)

At the 1820 and 1826 general elections, Matthias Attwood was elected Conservative MP for the Borough of Callington, Cornwall. In 1830 and 1831, he successfully contested Boroughbridge, Yorkshire. Following the abolition of his constituency in the Reform Act of 1832, Attwood was accepted as member in the newly created Borough of Whitehaven, Cumberland, being returned there without opposition in the elections of 1832, 1835, 1837 and 1841. He retired from Parliament in 1847.

Attwood lived at Muswell Hill in the 1830s and at Manor Park, Streatham in the 1840s. About 1849 he moved to 169 Denmark Hill and died there on 11 November 1851. He is buried at Norwood Cemetery with his wife, Susannah, who had died in 1842. He was survived by his only son, Matthias Wolverley Attwood.

## Matthias Wolverley Attwood (1808-65)
## 169 Denmark Hill
## MP and Businessman

The only child of Matthias Attwood, Matthias Wolverley Attwood became a merchant in London. A bachelor, he lived with his parents at Manor Park, Streatham in the 1840s and 169 Denmark Hill from c1849.

Matthias was elected Conservative MP for Greenwich in 1837. However, he was defeated in each of the three elections of 1841: first in the City of London, second at Kinsale and finally at Sunderland.

On the death of his father in 1851, he inherited 169 Denmark Hill and his father's shares in the bank of Spooner, Attwood and Co. From his father he also took over the chairmanship of the General Steam Navigation Company, which Matthias senior had helped to establish. He was also Deputy Lieutenant for Middlesex and a JP.

In 1863 he came into a large sum of money when Spooner, Attwood and Co. was taken over by Barclay, Bevan, Tritton and Co. On his death, 17 September 1865, he left nearly £900,000 and 169 Denmark Hill to his uncle, Benjamin Atwood. He is buried in his parents' grave at Norwood Cemetery.

## Charles Baily (1815-78)
## The Triangle, Denmark Hill
## Architect

Charles Baily was born 10 April 1815 at 71 Gracechurch Street in the City of London and christened at the nearby church of St Margaret Pattens in Rood Lane. He was the third son of William Baily and his wife, Susanna.

Charles trained as an architect, working in practices in Newark and Lincoln. Later he was appointed Principal Assistant to the London City Architect, where he helped lead construction of the new Guildhall roof and of the Corporation Library.

When, in the 1850s Charles moved from Lincoln back to London, he took up residence at 67 Camberwell Grove. However, by 1861 he was living at a house, later 151 Denmark Hill, located where the Fox-on-the-Hill pub is today.

Charles' independent work included St John's Church in Goose Green, East Dulwich, completed in 1865, as well as restoring Barnard's Inn Hall and Leigh Church (with a new tower), near Tunbridge Wells, Kent. He also worked on St George's Hall and the Liverpool Assize Courts.

On 2 October 1878, after a violent illness lasting several weeks, Charles committed suicide at his house in Reigate, squeezing through an upper floor window that was only 15" (36cm) wide, then falling 20' to the ground. He was survived by his wife Frances and four children. He is buried in Norwood Cemetery.

## Rt Hon. George Nicoll Barnes (1859-1940)
## 76 Herne Hill
## Trade Unionist and Politician

George Nicoll Barnes was born 2 January 1859 at Lochee, Forfarshire. He was the second of five sons of James Barnes, engineer and millman, and his wife Catherine.

George began his working life aged eleven at a jute mill managed by his father at Ponders End, Middlesex. He served his engineering apprenticeship at Powis James of Lambeth and then worked at Parker's foundry in Dundee and at Vickers in Barrow. In 1879 he returned to London and found work at Lucas and Airds in Fulham.

In 1882 he married Jessie Langlands. They had two sons and a daughter. George became an active trade unionist in the Amalgamated Society of Engineers (ASE) and a committee member of the Cooperative movement; and he helped form the Independent Labour Party (ILP) in 1893.

In 1896 he became a full-time trade union official on being elected Secretary of the ASE. This made him one of the country's most powerful labour leaders. In July 1897 George led the ASE in a long strike aimed at winning an eight-hour day; it ended unsuccessfully the following January. However, the Employers Federation did agree to negotiate wages and conditions with the ASE. He resigned as General Secretary in 1908.

George was a committed socialist; he was convinced that real progress on employees' pay and conditions would be made only if more trade unionist MPs could be elected. He stood unsuccessfully as ILP parliamentary candidate for the seat of Rochdale in 1895. However, at the 1906 general election he was one of 29 ILP candidates who were elected to Parliament, representing Glasgow Blackfriars.

As an MP, George was a key spokesman for the labour position on Old Age Pensions and National Insurance. In 1910 he became chairman of the Parliamentary Labour Party. In 1914 he strongly supported Britain's involvement in WW1. The death of his youngest son Henry (known by the family as Dick), killed aged 26 on the Western Front in September 1915, did not affect his views; and in 1916 he was one of the few Labour MPs to support conscription. That December he was invited to join the war cabinet, becoming the first Minister of Pensions and sitting on the government committee for war pensions. In August 1917 he became Minister without Portfolio, representing the interests of organised labour, and was responsible for a sympathetic government enquiry into the industrial unrest of that year.

George was Labour's only representative at the Paris Peace Conference. He used his position to argue against excessive reparations and to promote the rights of working people. His ideas formed the basis of Part 13 of the Treaty of Versailles. He attended the first Assembly of the League of Nations in 1920, and helped form the ILO (International Labour Organization) as an agency of the League.

At the end of the war, however, the Labour Party had withdrawn from Lloyd George's coalition government. George resigned from the party to remain as Minister of Pensions. Surviving a challenge from an official Labour Party candidate in the 1918 general election, he kept his ministerial post until resigning for health reasons in January 1920, when he was made a Companion of Honour. George remained a backbencher until, being unable to obtain support from the Labour Party for the 1922 general election, he left Parliament.

He had an active retirement, working in the ILO and publishing several books. These included his 1923 autobiography, *From Workshop to War Cabinet* and the 1926 *History of the International Labour Office.*

George Barnes lived at 76 Herne Hill from 1918 until his death on 21 April 1940. He is buried in Fulham Cemetery.

## Sir Frederick Barthorpe (1857-1942) 217 Norwood Road and 78 Herne Hill Alderman and Banker

In 1915, Frederick James Barthorpe was appointed Chief Joint General Manager of the London County & Westminster Bank Ltd., the forerunner of the NatWest Bank. This was after having served the bank as Secretary (from 1903) and Head Office Manager (from 1909). He was also Chairman of the Marconi Code Company, a Fellow and past-President of the Chartered Institute of Secretaries and a Fellow of the Institute of Bankers. During his career, he published two books: *Consuls and the Sinking Fund* and *Indian Currency – its first and second lines of defence*.

Born in Pimlico, at the time of the 1881 census he was a 24 year old bank clerk living with his widowed mother and younger brother John, at 11 Park Villa, now 217 Norwood Road. In 1910, aged 53, he married Maria Evelyn Cuyper, 22; they had one son. The couple lived at 2 Herne Hill Mansions, moving in 1913 to 78 Herne Hill at the corner with Gubyon Avenue. Their final home, from c1924, was a large detached house called Woodlawns, 16 Leigham Court Road, Streatham.

In 1911 Frederick retired from the 4th (City of London) Battalion of the London Regiment Royal Fusiliers, where he had risen to the rank of Major. At the beginning of WW1, he assisted in the formation of the 26th (Service) Battalion of the Royal Fusiliers (Bankers' Battalion).

In 1921, Frederick became Alderman of the City of London for Bread Street Ward. He was knighted by King George V in 1925 after serving as Sheriff for a year. Other honours included, from the Pope, Knight Commander of the Order of St Gregory the Great, for services to the Roman Catholic Church (he was a devout Catholic) and the Legion of Honour from President Doumergue of France.

Sir Frederick died 28 February 1942 at Streatham and is buried with his mother (d 1905) and wife (d 1931) in Norwood Cemetery.

## Edwin Bartlett (1845-86) 301/303 Railton Road Shopkeeper and Murder Victim

Edwin Bartlett was a partner in the prosperous firm of Baxter & Bartlett, grocers and cheese-mongers, with shops in Lordship Lane, East Dulwich and at 1-2 Station Road, later to become 301/303 Railton Road following street renaming.

In 1875 he met and married Adelaide Blanche de la Tremouille, a very attractive French woman from Orléans, who was staying with an aunt and uncle in Kingston-upon-Thames. At the time of their marriage Edwin was 29 and Adelaide 19. They went to live in a flat over the Herne Hill shop, though Adelaide spent most of the next two years at a boarding school in Stoke Newington, then at a finishing school in Belgium.

Edwin seems to have had little interest in sex - according to Adelaide, she and her husband had sexual intercourse only once during their married life.

Although she became pregnant, the baby died in childbirth. Not long after her coming to live permanently in Herne Hill, Adelaide's father-in-law accused her of an affair with Edwin's brother, Frederick. This she strenuously denied; the accusation was later formally withdrawn.

In 1883 the Bartletts went to live above the shop in Lordship Lane. Two years later the couple moved to Merton Abbey, where they met a 27 year old Wesleyan minister, George Dyson, with whom they became very friendly. An affectionate relationship developed between Adelaide and the clergyman. Edwin did not object and even encouraged Dyson to visit and instruct Adelaide in Latin, mathematics, history and geography. During these visits the curtains were often closed; they were several times discovered in potentially compromising positions.

In August 1885 the Bartletts moved into furnished rooms at 85 Claverton Street, Pimlico. By this time they were sleeping in separate bedrooms. This was possibly because of Edwin's foul-smelling breath - some years previously he had had all his teeth sawn off at the gums, which must have resulted in serious decay and hence severe halitosis. Very soon after the move to Pimlico Edwin became ill, the doctor diagnosing "sub acute gastritis". A dentist removed his decayed teeth and stumps; but Edwin remained depressed.

On 27 December 1885 Adelaide asked Reverend Dyson to buy her some chloroform, which he did, from chemists in Putney and in Wimbledon. As well as an anaesthetic, chloroform was then used as a liniment to ease rheumatic pains and as a stain remover. However, it can be dangerous; liquid chloroform burns the skin, and a small dose can cause sudden death by stopping the heart. Any substantial amount taken orally is likely to be lethal.

Early on New Year's Day 1886, Adelaide roused neighbours to say she had awoken to find Edwin dead. The subsequent autopsy found Edwin's stomach to contain liquid chloroform; this was later confirmed as the cause of death. No traces of chloroform were found in Edwin's mouth or throat. Nevertheless, the coroner's jury gave a verdict of wilful murder against Adelaide. Dyson was later arrested and charged with being an accessory before the fact, though the case against him was later withdrawn.

At her trial the following April, Adelaide was defended by one of the greatest advocates of the time, the renowned barrister Edward Clarke QC MP. Clarke based his case largely on the lack of evidence on how the chloroform had been administered. The expert witnesses could not explain how it had got into Edwin's stomach without leaving tell-tale signs of burning in his throat or windpipe. Despite the judge's obvious belief in Adelaide's guilt, the jury quickly decided that she was innocent. But in announcing the verdict, the jury foreman stated, "Although we think there is the gravest suspicion attaching to the prisoner, we do not think there is sufficient evidence to show how or by whom the chloroform was administered."

After the trial, Dyson disappeared. Adelaide returned to Orléans, and may later have emigrated to America. Queen Victoria's surgeon at St Bartholomew's Hospital, Sir James Paget, afterwards said "Now the case is over, she should tell us in the interests of science how she did it."

Bartlett's Railton Road shop was completely destroyed in an air-raid on 16 October 1940, along with a number of neighbouring properties.

## John Belcher (1841-1913)
## 2 Champion Hill
## Architect

John Belcher was born on the 10th July 1841 at 3 Montague Terrace (now 8 Brockham Street), Southwark, the eldest of ten children. Like his father, John Belcher Sr (1817-90), he became an architect, studying in Luxembourg and Paris before becoming a partner in John Sr's practice in 1865. John soon took over most of the design work, and followed his father into the Catholic Apostolic Church, where he became a Minister. John was also a cellist and a keen amateur singer, an accomplished bass; he at one time contemplated a musical career.

In his youth John Belcher showed an enthusiasm for the Gothic style. However, he never felt bound by tradition or convention and was quick to react to new movements. Having the courage of his convictions he readily responded to changing styles and tastes, such as when Italian renaissance began to replace the English Gothic revival. He was particularly enthused by the palaces of Genoa, giving him the opportunity to use sculpture and mural decoration in the classic tradition. His designs represent the architectural response to the arts and crafts movement of the late 19th century.

Belcher was a talented and original architect whose work was well regarded. For two years, from 1904, he was President of the Royal Institute of British Architects (RIBA), elected an Associate of the Royal Academy (ARA) in 1900 and a Royal Academician (RA) in 1909. In 1907 he was awarded the prestigious RIBA gold medal. By 1906 Belcher's ill health meant that most of the design work was being handled by his partner, John James Joass (1868-1952). Both Joass and Pite later admitted they did their best designs when working with Belcher.

Belcher was responsible for many public and domestic buildings, most of which survive. Amongst his architectural achievements are the Mappin and Webb building, Poultry (1871 - sadly demolished in 1994); the Catholic Apostolic Church, Camberwell New Road (1875 - now St Mary's Greek Orthodox Cathedral); the offices of the Institute of Chartered Accountants, Moorgate (1892, with his good friend the architect Arthur Beresford Pite); Colchester Town Hall (1898); Electra House, Finsbury Pavement (1902 - now City of London University); The Ashton Memorial, Lancaster (1906), and Whiteley's store, Bayswater (1910). Although never built, his 1891 design for the Victoria and Albert Museum added to Belcher's reputation and was a turning point for the revival of the English Baroque style.

Belcher designed the house Redholm, 2 Champion Hill, located next door to the Fox-on-the-Hill, where he lived from 1885 until his death. For many years (1950s-1970s) the ground floor of the house was used as a public bar for the pub next door. However, it is now converted to flats and except for the loss of a chimney stack and shortening of two others, it is substantially the same as when first built. The house was listed Grade II in 1988.

He was married in 1865 to Florence, daughter of Matthew Parker, a Dublin minister; they had no children. John Belcher died 8 November 1913 at Redholm and was buried in Norwood Cemetery.

## Frederick William Benecke (c1802-65) - Merchant and Henriette Elisabeth Benecke (c1809-93), 174 Denmark Hill

Frederick Benecke and his wife Henriette were born in Germany but became naturalised British subjects when they settled here. Frederick described himself as a general merchant, and was a partner in the firm of Schunck, Souchay & Co. of 8 Tokenhouse Yard and later, 63 Moorgate Street in the City of London. About 1835, the family, which eventually comprised four sons and six daughters, moved from Deptford to 174 Denmark Hill, a large house (demolished c1906) at a site now in Ruskin Park at the corner with Ferndene Road. This was an area where many German families lived.

***Sundial Pedestal in Ruskin Park***

***Felix Mendelssohn Bartholdy***

Henriette Benecke was the aunt of Cecile Mendelssohn (1817-53), née Jeanrenaud, wife of the composer Felix Mendelssohn Bartholdy (1809-47). In May 1842 the Mendelssohns came to London and stayed with the Benecke family for several weeks. Reminiscing on their visit many years later, Henriette remembered one particular day when the two families went on a picnic to Windsor, but Mendelssohn stayed behind:

> On the long drive to Windsor Mrs. Benecke said to Frau Mendelssohn: 'Why did not Felix come with us today?' She replied, 'I think that Felix has something in his mind that he wants to write down.' 'But,' said her hostess, 'there is nothing for his dinner, only cold meat and rice milk - just the children's dinner.' 'Oh never mind' replied Frau M; 'he likes nothing better than rice milk. He will be all right.' On their return home, Mendelssohn, full of spirits, was waiting in the garden-drive to receive them, and greeted them with a hearty welcome. When they were assembled in his temporary study he played the lovely *Lied in A*, saying, 'This is what I have been doing while you have been away.'

The *Lied in A* was briefly called *Camberwell Green* but is now known as *Chanson de Printemps* or *Spring Song* from Mendelssohn's *Songs without Words* Opus 62 No. 6. Mrs Benecke went on to recall that Mendelssohn:

> ...was fond of romping with the children, and they with him; and the quaver rests in the bass...and the frequent staccato notes in the treble, represent the constant withdrawal of his hands from the pianoforte in order to defend himself against the repeated attacks of the little ones, who, being alone with him, wanted to drag him away from the pianoforte and into the garden for a romp. The autographed MS is dated 'London, June 1, 1842,' the day of the picnic.

When Ruskin Park opened in 1907, the site of the house was marked by a sundial to commemorate Mendelssohn's visit. However, all that remains today is the terracotta pedestal, decorated with Tudor roses.

On 8 August 1865, Frederick Benecke died at the Europäischer Hotel, Heidelberg while on a visit to Germany. He left £120,000 in his will. Henriette died 29 January 1893. Four of her children, Eliza, Ernest, Alice and Cecile, continued to live at 174 Denmark Hill. In 1906 the house was demolished to create Ruskin Park and the Beneckes moved to 182 Denmark Hill. Ernest, the last surviving Benecke at Denmark Hill died in 1924. Henriette, Eliza, Ernest and Alice are buried in Norwood Cemetery.

## Otto Benecke (c1837-1922)
## 174 and 184 Denmark Hill
## Treasurer of Camberwell Dispensary

Otto August Benecke was the third son of Frederick and Henriette Benecke. Like his older brother, Charles Victor, he grew up at 174 Denmark Hill and followed his father into business as a merchant trader. In 1862 at St Matthew's Church, Denmark Hill, he married Ada Maria Rhodes, the daughter of Charles Henry Rhodes, a solicitor of 210 Denmark Hill. The couple lived for a time with Otto's parents, moving in the 1870s to Cedar Lodge, 184 Denmark Hill (now demolished) on the site of the present 170 Denmark Hill, built in the 1940s. There is still a Cedar of Lebanon tree in the front garden. About 1897 Benecke retired to Eastbourne where he died on 2 May 1922.

In those days, it was common for people in the prosperous middle classes to give their services free for charitable work helping the poor. For a time Otto Benecke was Treasurer of the Camberwell Provident Dispensary at 325 Camberwell New Road where part of a stone plaque can still be read:

Founded 1862.
Rebuilt by voluntary contributions
1880.
Charles Druce, President.
Otto A. Benecke, Treasurer

The Dispensary, a type of 'sick club', assisted poor people living within a radius of 1¼ miles of St Giles' Church, when they became ill. At the same time, it encouraged habits of discipline and independence. To qualify as a member, weekly earnings had to be 30 shillings (£1.50) or less and small monthly payments of 2d (0.8p) to 8d (3.2p) were required. Records for 1873 show that there were over 6,000 members; about 14,000 consultations at the Dispensary; over 7,000 visits to patients in their own homes. In attendance were six doctors and one dentist. The Dispensary did sterling work in the community until the founding of the National Health Service in 1948. Later the Dispensary building became an estate agent's office, an art gallery and now (2006) a restaurant.

## Victor Benecke (c1831-1908)
## 174 Denmark Hill
## Merchant and Mendelssohn's Son-in-Law

Charles Victor Benecke was the eldest son of Frederick and Henriette Benecke, who from the late 1830s lived at 174 Denmark Hill. Victor followed his father into business as a merchant trader with the firm of Messrs. Schunck, Souchay & Co. About 1861, at Frankfurt-am-Main, he married Marie Pauline Helene Mendelssohn (c1840-98), daughter of the composer Felix Mendelssohn Bartholdy. On their return to London, the couple lived with his parents, later moving to a house called Highwood at Roehampton. There they brought up their two sons and two daughters.

The eldest son, Paul Victor Mendelssohn Benecke, MA (1868-1944) became a Fellow of Magdalen College, Oxford, spending the rest of his days there, a confirmed bachelor. He occupied the same set of rooms for 53 years and was Home Bursar to the College for 20 years. He was, by all accounts, a first class amateur pianist. The second son, Edward Felix Mendelssohn Benecke (1870-95) was educated at Balliol College, Oxford but perished in a climbing accident in Switzerland.

***James Bennett standing centre with the Derby School orchestra***

After the death of his wife in 1898, Victor moved with his two daughters to Church House, Brasted in Kent where he died 24 October 1908.

## James Sterndale Bennett (1847-1928) 147 Denmark Hill Headmaster and Biographer

The second son of composer Sir William Sterndale Bennett (1816-75), James Robert Sterndale Bennett was educated at Kensington School and St John's College, Cambridge where he read mathematics. However, perhaps naturally, music was his first love and interest. He became a teacher, first as assistant master at Sherbourne School and later as mathematics lecturer at King's College, London. He also lectured on acoustics at the Royal Academy of Music. In 1876 James married Mabel Agnes Gaskell; they had seven children. About 1888 they lived at 147 Denmark Hill (now demolished) situated at the junction with Champion Hill.

In 1889 James was appointed Headmaster of Derby School, where he devoted much energy to developing the musical side of the school curriculum. After ten years at Derby he retired early with the set purpose of writing his father's biography, *The Life of William Sterndale Bennett*, published 1907. Apart from a few contributions to *Grove's Dictionary of Music and Musicians,* this biography was his only published work. He died 4 June 1928 at Dymchurch in Kent.

## Sir Henry Bessemer (1813-98) 165 Denmark Hill Engineer and Inventor

Sir Henry Bessemer, one of this country's greatest inventors and innovators, was born 19 January 1813, in Charlton, near Hitchin, Hertfordshire. He joined his father's engineering and type-founding business, quickly showing considerable mechanical skills and inventiveness. His first major invention was a way of using brass powder as an additive to produce 'gold' paint. For 40 years the process was kept secret from competitors with, for much of this time, only himself and three of his wife's brothers allowed access. Paint made with his secret formula was used on much of the gilded decoration of the time and brought him great wealth.

Between 1838 and 1883 Bessemer was granted 118 patents. These covered a wide range of products, such as a train braking system, an improved method of extracting sugar from sugar-cane and a process for improving optical glass. Despite many important and profitable discoveries, Bessemer is best known for his invention in the 1850s of the 'Bessemer Converter'. This is a process where air is blown through molten pig iron, to produce steel by removing impurities such as carbon and sulphur. This invention, described as "the most important event of its kind in history", revolutionised steel production. Although later superseded by the open hearth process, it enabled good quality steel to be produced cheaply and in large quantities, resulting in great improvements to armaments manufacture, ship building, railways and civil engineering materials.

As well as his knighthood, awarded in 1879, Bessemer's many honours included a Fellowship of the Royal Society and the Royal Society of Arts' gold medal. Not all Bessemer's inventions were successful; his swinging saloon for seagoing ships to reduce seasickness proved impracticable.

He retired in 1856 and set up as a consultant. With the money from his patent royalties he bought, in 1863, a 40 acre (17 hectare) estate on Denmark Hill. There he demolished an existing house and built a new one to the designs of Charles Barry Jr, calling it Bessemer House.

A few years later he built a house next door for his daughter Elizabeth (1834-1915) and her husband William Wright (1827-1908).

The houses eventually became respectively Nos. 165 and 167 Denmark Hill. Features of his estate included a lake, a model farm, an underground cavern and an observatory with, then, the world's second largest telescope.

Sir Henry Bessemer died 15 March 1898 and was buried in Norwood Cemetery; his grave is Grade II listed. Both houses were eventually turned into hotels. However, they were demolished in 1947 to make way for the present houses and blocks of flats and the Bessemer Grange School.

## Algernon Sidney Bicknell (1832-1911) 5 Herne Hill Traveller, Author and Scientist

It has been said that Sidney Bicknell was "a lout". However, most saw him as a highly intelligent and adventurous traveller and mountaineer.

The son of Elhanan Bicknell and his third wife, Lucinda, Algernon was born in Herne Hill 9 October 1832.

His father's wealth gave him independent means, so Sidney was able to devote himself to travel, mountaineering and scientific studies. He made ten ascents of Vesuvius, six during eruptions, traversed the Andes four times and crossed South America through the Amazonian jungle. Touring Italy, he was in Naples at the time of Garibaldi's entry and saw the Battle of the Volturno, later publishing an account of his experiences. He was also witness to many of the Franco-Prussian battles, and was one of the first Englishmen to make an ascent in a balloon.

In 1857, Sidney married Rosa Wild and set up home at Stapleford Place in Sussex. There he built an observatory to study astronomy. He also developed an extensive library, and published a book on his research into fungi. His last home was Barcombe House, Barcombe, Sussex.

A member of several scientific societies, Sidney was elected a Fellow of the Linnaean Society and Royal Astronomical Society. He also studied archaeology, and at the time of his death was engaged in writing on this subject. He was an enthusiastic photographer and took several photographs dating from 1859 of the Bicknell mansion and its grounds. He also took an interest in family history and published a book, *Five Pedigrees,* on the remarkable Bicknell family.

Algernon Sidney Bicknell died in Brighton 26 October 1911, following an operation. He was survived by his wife, two sons and four daughters.

## Clarence Bicknell (1842-1918) 5 Herne Hill - Botanist and Archaeologist

Clarence Bicknell was born 27 October 1842, the youngest son of Elhanan Bicknell and his wife Lucinda. The family lived at 5 Herne Hill opposite the present Dorchester Court; they were neighbours of John Ruskin. Clarence was brought up in a middle class, liberal, happy home where appreciation of the arts was encouraged by his father's friendship with the British painters Turner, Landseer and David Roberts.

In 1862 Clarence went up to Trinity College, Cambridge, where he read mathematics. After graduating in 1865 he took holy orders in the Church of England. He became a curate in Walworth, Southwark, where he lived a simple life, giving his income to the poor. After leaving Walworth he lived with friends in the enclosed order, Brotherhood of the Holy Spirit, in Stoke-by-Terne, Shropshire. However, after some years he began to have serious religious doubts and decided to use his wealth to travel the world.

In 1878 Clarence visited Bordighera on the Italian 'coast of flowers'. Here he developed his interest in botany, studying the local flora and natural history. He decided to settle there, ministering to the British community and creating the Bicknell Museum, which housed his books and was used as a meeting place for the local community to pursue cultural and intellectual interests. Clarence was an enthusiast for Esperanto, a vegetarian, against the water closet in the cause of organic husbandry, and a believer in washing in mountain streams.

Clarence published the results of his studies of alpine plants and rock engravings in Italian scientific journals, based on his collections of rubbings, drawings and photographs. In 1885 he published *Flowering Plants and Ferns of the Riviera and adjoining Mountains*, which he illustrated. Also in that year he sketched 50 of the mysterious prehistoric designs along the western edge of Mount Bordighera. In 1896 he published *Flora of Bordighera and San Remo*, followed by a book on the local rock engravings at Mount Bego (1913).

Clarence Bicknell never married. He died on 17 July 1918 at his house, Casa Fontanalba. In 1916, plaques to honour his work were placed on his house and on the rock face at Las Mesches, the gateway to Mount Bego. In 1973 a sub-species of the giant knapweed, a speciality of the alpine area, was named Leuzea Rhapontica Bicknellii.

## Elhanan Bicknell (1788-1861)
## 5 Herne Hill
## Art Patron and Businessman

Elhanan Bicknell, named after celebrated American preacher Elhanan Winchester, was born 21 December 1788 at 8 Blackman Street, Southwark. He was the second son of William Bicknell (1749–1825) and his wife Elizabeth (1756–1821). William, a serge manufacturer, sold his business to set up a school, which he moved to Tooting Common in 1804. There Elhanan was educated and also taught for a while. In 1808 he went to Shropshire to learn farming. However, the following year he was invited to become a partner, with his cousin John Bicknell Langton, in his uncle's ship-owning, whaling and candle-manufacturing business, at 3 High Street, Newington Butts. The firm, known from the 1820s as Langton and Bicknell, quickly expanded. It eventually owned more than 30 ships, and for a time monopolised the Pacific sperm-whale fishery. With the advent of free trade, which Elhanan supported, their monopoly was lost.

In 1819 Elhanan moved to a simple late Georgian building in extensive grounds, near what is now the junction of Danecroft Road and Herne Hill, opposite the present Dorchester Court. It was to be Elhanan's home for the rest of his life, during which time the house was extended and a conservatory added.

As well as being an astute businessman Elhanan had a natural gift for judging paintings and modern sculpture. Over the next 40 years he built up a huge collection of the finest British contemporary art. His collection eventually represented all the major artists of the day, including Turner, Gainsborough, Roberts, Wilson, Copley and Landseer. His house was always open to artists and art connoisseurs; regular visitors included John Ruskin. Elhanan was one of four principal collectors of modern British art (Vernon, Wells and Sheepshanks being the others) described in an article in the *Athenaeum* magazine as "men uninspired by motives of profit and investment (who) collected art because of the painter's skill and because of the pleasure and instruction they derived from their contemplation".

Elhanan Bicknell was a progressive liberal and principal contributor to the building of the Unitarian chapel at Brixton. He married four times: first, on 16 October 1810, to Hannah Wootton Langton (d 1815) the sister of his business partner. With Hannah he had a son, also Elhanan. His second marriage, on 13 February 1817, to Mary Jones (d 1827), produced another son, Henry Sanford. His third marriage, to Lucinda Sarah Knight Browne (d 1850) was held on 5 May 1829; their eight children included Herman, the Orientalist, Algernon Sidney, the traveller and adventurer, and Clarence, the botanist. Lucinda was the sister of Phiz, the illustrator of Charles Dickens' novels. Elhanan's last wife was a widow, Louisa Holland Jones (c1803-84), whom he married on 14 August 1851.

By summer 1861, Elhanan's health was failing and he retired from business. He died, greatly lamented by his artists' circle, at his house on 27 November 1861 and was buried at Norwood Cemetery. He was survived by eleven of his children. His estate was valued at over £400,000. The house, later designated 5 Herne Hill, then named Carlton House, was demolished in the 1900s.

Elhanan Bicknell had wanted to leave his collection, which included 122 paintings, to the nation. But two years after his death it was broken up and sold, realising nearly £75,000 - the highest figure ever obtained at auction for English artistic work. A vast crowd came to view the collection; the row of carriages, more than a mile long, blocked the road.

## Henry Sanford Bicknell (1818-80)
## 5 Herne Hill
## Art Collector

Henry Sanford Bicknell was the fifth child of Elhanan Bicknell and his second wife, Mary Jones (d 1827). The family lived in a mansion which was numbered 5 Herne Hill.

In 1841 Henry married Christine Roberts (1821-72), the daughter of David Roberts RA, the artist and great friend of Elhanan Bicknell. The couple moved to live in Tulse Hill and later to Cavendish House, Clapham Park, where he died on 28 May 1880. The house was demolished in 1905.

Like his father, Henry was an art collector; and his collection included many paintings by his father-in-law. A year after his death the collection was sold for £24,330 at Christie's. In his will, Henry left £90,000. He was buried with his wife at Norwood Cemetery in the same grave as his father and father-in-law

## Herman Bicknell (1830-1875)
## 5 Herne Hill
## Traveller and Orientalist

> *Ala ya ayyuha's, Saki - pass round and offer thou the bowl,*
> *For love, which seemed at first so easy, has now brought trouble to my soul.*
>
> Hafiz, Ghazal no.1, couplet 1: translated by Herman Bicknell

Herman Bicknell was born at 5 Herne Hill 2 April 1830, the third surviving son of Elhanan Bicknell and his third wife, Lucinda. After studying at University College and St Bartholomew's Hospital, he joined the army in India in 1854 as Assistant-Surgeon. As well as being involved in the Indian Mutiny, he served in China, Java and Tibet. Soon after returning to England in 1860, he resigned his commission and spent the rest of his life in travel, mountaineering and the study of archaeology, botany and Oriental languages.

Herman's travels encompassed the Arctic, South America, Africa and the Near and Far East. A highly talented linguist, he became fluent in several oriental languages. In the early 1860s he lived for a long period in the native quarter of Cairo, becoming so familiar with Islamic culture that he was able to join the annual pilgrimage to Mecca; he was the first Englishman to do so undisguised. Later he was only the second Christian to enter (this time in disguise) the holy shrine of Fatima at Qum in Iran, closed to non-Muslims.

Herman made a particular study of the works of Hafiz, the 14th century Persian poet, and translated many of his poems into English. However, before he could complete his final manuscript, he died of cancer on 14 March 1875. It is said that his death was hastened by injuries sustained in an accident five years earlier, when he was nearly killed during an attempt to climb the Matterhorn. Fortunately his brother, Algernon Sidney Bicknell, organised the publication of the translations, in a beautifully produced book published 1875. Herman's last home was in Ramsgate, where he died and was buried.

## Frederick Bird (1858-1929)
## 2 Sunray Avenue
## Singer, Baker and Mayor

Born in Holborn, London, the son of a furniture and picture dealer, Frederick was educated at St Martin's School, Charing Cross. Aged nine he was found to have a beautiful boy-soprano voice. From 5,000 choristers at a concert at the Crystal Palace, he was singled out as a potential soloist by the eminent conductor and music teacher, John Hullah (1812-84). From then on, he was frequently in demand for ballad concerts conducted by Hullah, and in his twenties associated with the Christy Minstrels at St James' Hall.

Several of his family were bakers; in 1885 aged 29, he bought a baker's business at 16 Lebanon Street, Walworth (between Thurlow and Bagshot Streets). At the time of the 1891 census he was living with his wife Elizabeth, aged 33, and their daughter Maude. Being a successful baker, Bird joined the local association where his gentle reasoning abilities, tact and good judgement were soon noticed. In 1890 he was persuaded to take the vacant position of Secretary of the South London Council of Master Bakers, a post he held for over 25 years. A serious illness in 1897 forced him to sell his baker's shop. On recovering he became London agent and collector for a firm of coal merchants, Messrs Hoare, Gothard & Co. However he continued his support for the baking trade, spending much of his leisure time working for its advancement. His counsel was much in demand over the vexed question of price competition, and also in implementing the Underground Bakehouse Act, where the authorities had power to close all bakehouses below street level.

Politically he was a staunch Conservative, serving on the Newington Vestry for a few years and then, from 1900-28, as a Metropolitan Borough of Southwark Councillor, representing St Peter's Ward. He was elected Mayor 1917-18 and Alderman from 1928. Frederick supported many charities, serving on numerous committees. He had a particular interest in the provision of benefits to ex-servicemen and their families after WW1. He was teetotal, always an eloquent orator and for some years served as Chief Southwark Magistrate.

During the 1920s, Frederick lived with his son-in-law and daughter, Arthur and Maude Boddy, at 2 Sunray Avenue. He died 3 February 1929 and his burial took place at Norwood Cemetery after a service at St Matthew's Church, Denmark Hill; the site is now King's College Hospital School of Dental Surgery. At his funeral representatives from all political parties expressed their genuine sympathy and sorrow.

## Joshua John Blades Blackburn (1854-1898) Brockwell Hall

J J B Blackburn was born in Westminster in 1854, the eldest son of Joshua Blackburn and his wife Mary. In 1860 his father inherited Brockwell Hall and the surrounding estate and the family made a home there. In the 1881 census J J B Blackburn, aged 26, was still living at the Hall, identified as a student of law. However, he later

***Brockwell Hall***

went to live at Tregaron, Beckenham Road, Beckenham. In 1888 his father died and the Hall and much of the surrounding land were sold to create the public park. J J B, who inherited the remaining 43 acres (18 hectares) of the former estate, donated £2,000. He died whilst on a visit to Ramsgate, 23 November 1898, at the Rising Sun Hotel, survived by his wife Ellen Louise. He was buried in Norwood Cemetery.

Brockwell Park took on substantially its present form when in 1901 the remaining 43 acres were bought by the London County Council from J J B Blackburn's trustees.

## Joshua Blackburn (1822-88) Brockwell Hall

Joshua Blackburn Jr was the grandson of John Blades, the glass manufacturer who had built Brockwell Hall and laid out the surrounding park. In 1860, on the death of his mother Elizabeth, Joshua inherited the entire estate. Two years later Herne Hill Station opened, creating an increased demand for housing in the area. Taking advantage of this, Joshua built a line of houses near the site of the present Brockwell Park changing rooms. He also built Brockwell House, located between the present BMX track and the Hall. In 1862 he donated the land and contributed to the cost of the new St Jude's Church in Dulwich Road. He doubtless thought a church in the centre of the new neighbourhood would encourage further demand for development in the area.

Unfortunately Joshua's activities came to a halt when he became ill and was confined to a lunatic asylum. He died 18 December 1888 at Brockwell House and was buried in Norwood Cemetery. After Joshua's death, 78 acres (33 hectares) of his estate was sold, realising £117,000, to become the basis for what is now Brockwell Park. The remaining 43 acres passed to his son, J J B Blackburn. In 1901 the LCC bought this land and incorporated it to produce Brockwell Park substantially as we know it today.

## John Blades (1751-1829)
## Brockwell Hall
## Glassware Manufacturer

John Blades' legacy to Herne Hill, Brockwell Hall and the surrounding park, has given us our most important and valuable asset.

John Blades was a successful and wealthy glass manufacturer, glass merchant and exporter. His speciality was hand-blown, heavily cut and often very elaborate Georgian and Regency glassware. Blades opened his showrooms at 5 Ludgate Hill in 1783 and kept the business there until his death. He was known as "the great glass man of Ludgate Hill". His was the first English glass company to open a branch in Calcutta. By the time he married in 1789, he had been appointed Cut Glass Manufacturer to King George III. He also held a Royal Warrant to the Persian court.

His success was such that in 1809 he was able to buy the then Brockwell Hall and over 60 acres of surrounding land. At that time the Hall stood at the bottom of the hill, close to the present Rosendale Road entrance to the Park. Two years later, Blades demolished the old house and built a new Brockwell Hall, designed by J B Papworth, at the top of the hill. He laid out the surrounding fields as a private park and built houses in Brixton Water Lane for estate staff. They are still standing. In 1825 he built Clarence Lodge for one his daughters, Caroline Prodgers, wife of Rev. Edwyn Prodgers, the first vicar of St Matthew's Church, Brixton. The lodge stood on the site of the BMX track. Three years later he began work on a street of houses, Brockwell Terrace, on the site of the Lido. However, development stopped in 1829 when Blades died.

John Blades was buried in the family vault in the crypt of St Bride's Church, Fleet Street. Under his will, he left Clarence Lodge to his daughter Caroline and Brockwell Hall to his other daughter, Elizabeth Blackburn, wife of Joshua Blackburn. On their deaths, the whole of the estate was to pass to his grandson, also called Joshua Blackburn. Brockwell Hall is now Grade II* listed.

## Sir Edward Hardman Bowers (1854-1914)
## 24 Stradella Road
## Inland Revenue Chief Inspector

Born in Drogheda, Ireland, Edward Hardman Bowers was a career Civil Servant. At the age of 18 he started work as Assistant Surveyor of Taxes; he stayed in the Inland Revenue for the rest of his career, working his way up the ladder. In 1910 he was appointed

Chief Inspector of the Tax Surveying Branch, at an annual salary of £1,200 - equivalent to some £80,000 today, but worth rather more with income tax then at only 9d in the £ (3.75%). This position he held until his death. His responsibilities included collecting stamp duties, income tax, land and property tax and estate duties. He was knighted in 1913.

Edward's principal leisure interest was breeding bull dogs. He was a founder member, Secretary and Treasurer of the British Bulldog Club, and co-author of the book *Bull Dog Pedigrees*. This three-volume opus, published between 1892 and 1898, lists some 10,250 bulldogs registered with the Kennel Club, along with their pedigrees, owners and other details. The prefaces to each volume are largely devoted to complaints about the Kennel Club's activities.

Edward married Margaret Jones in 1880; they had a son and a daughter. In 1901 or 1902 they moved to a newly built house at 24 Stradella Road and lived there until Sir Edward's death on 19 April 1914.

## John Braham (1777-1856)
## Herne Hill Cottage
## Singer

Abraham (John) Braham was born in London, most probably on 20 March 1777, though some accounts give his date of birth as 1774. Taught singing by an uncle, he made his first public appearance at Covent Garden 21 April 1787. When his voice broke John, his parents having died, had to support himself by giving piano lessons. However, after a few years he developed an exceptionally pure and rich tenor voice and made a second debut in 1794 in Bath.

In 1796 he reappeared in London at Drury Lane in Joseph Storace's opera *Mahmoud*. This was so successful that further engagements followed; and in 1897 with the popular soprano Anna Storace, with whom he had established a relationship, he set out for Italy. On the way the couple spent eight months giving concerts in Paris, where they sang before Napoleon and Josephine.

In Italy he received a triumphal reception, appearing in all the main opera houses: Milan, Genoa, Leghorn and Venice, before returning to London in 1801. John appeared again at Covent Garden, proving so popular that, although scheduled to return to Vienna after a year, he decided to remain in England. In May 1802 Anna and John had a son, William.

After Anna's retirement from singing in 1809, the family moved to her house, Herne Hill Cottage. John continued his career, spending less and less time at home, until finally moving out in 1815 following an affair with Mrs Henry Wright. In July 1816, Mr Wright brought an action against John for criminal conversation (a phrase usually employed to denote the crime of adultery) and was awarded £1,000 in damages. John did not stay long with Mrs Wright, as on 11 November 1816 he married the stage-struck and much younger beauty Frances (Fanny) Elizabeth Bolton (1799-1846). Between 1819 and 1829, John and Fanny had six surviving children. In addition, John had taken responsibility for his son William, after Anna Storace's death in 1817.

During his peak years, John commanded enormous fees and became very wealthy. In 1809 he sang for 15 nights at the Theatre Royal, Dublin, for the unparalleled sum of 2,000 guineas. Composing and teaching brought additional income. However, his talents as a businessman did not equal those as a singer. He made some catastrophic investments; and Fanny's theatrical enthusiasms and extravagances exacerbated the situation. At least twice, in 1849 and again in 1853, he was forced to go abroad to avoid his creditors and possible imprisonment for debt. John's financial difficulties meant he had to continue his singing career well beyond the time he would have liked to have retired. His last public appearance was at a concert in March 1852. With over 60 years between his first and final public performances, during 40 of which he was at the forefront of his profession, he must have been unique as a first rank singer. John died on 17 February 1856 at his home in Hanover Square, London and was buried in Kensal Green Cemetery.

Herne Hill Cottage, which had 13 rooms and stood in four acres, no longer exists; it was located where 5 Dorchester Drive now stands. In 1823, John James Ruskin moved into a house built in the grounds.

## William Brindley (1832-1919)
## 214 Denmark Hill
## Architectural Sculptor

The 1861 census shows William Brindley aged 28, born in Derby, married with two young daughters, living at Kelham near Newark-on-Trent, Nottinghamshire and working as an architectural sculptor. A few years later he moved to London and joined fellow Derby-born sculptor, William Farmer (1823-79) who had started a business in c1856 at 63 Westminster Bridge Road (then known as 4 Mead Place) in Lambeth. By c1868 they had become business partners.

The firm of Farmer & Brindley provided ornamental and decorative features such as cornices, friezes, panels and tracery, as well as statues, in stone, terracotta, wood, plaster and metal. William Farmer and William Brindley worked well as a team, with Brindley being the principal carver, very often working on-site, but under the direction of Farmer, who handled

***Ruskin Memorial in St Paul's Church***

the contracts. The architect George Gilbert Scott (1811-78) considered Brindley "the best carver I have met with and the one who best understands my view."

Farmer & Brindley produced architectural carvings for many prestigious projects by Scott. These included Lichfield Cathedral (finished 1884), the Foreign Office, Whitehall (1863-69), the Albert memorial (1863-72), the University of Glasgow (1864-70) and restoration projects at Exeter, Worcester and Gloucester Cathedrals. Other significant works included Holborn Viaduct (1863-69) under William Heywood, Manchester Town Hall (1868-77) and the Natural History Museum (1873-81) under Alfred Waterhouse (1830-1905). There were also collaborations on designs with architects G E Street, G F Bodley, R Norman Shaw and Sir Thomas Jackson.

William Brindley was a great searcher among books and art collections for ideas and details, visiting most of the important libraries and museums in Europe. His many travels to the Far East included three visits to Japan. William Farmer died in 1879 and Brindley ran the business alone for many years. Two well-known sculptors learned their craft at Farmer & Brindley. Harry Bates (1850-99) was apprenticed there for ten years in the 1870s; and Charles John Allen (1862-1955) worked there for ten years in the 1880s, training at Lambeth School of Art.

In the late 1870s, Brindley moved his home from next to the workshops to a detached house called Pergola, 214 Denmark Hill, demolished in the early 1900s. In the 1920s, 224 and 226 Denmark Hill were built on the site. About 1895 he moved to 41 Courtfield Road, South Kensington and later to St Johns Road, Boscombe near Bournemouth, where he died on 10 February 1919.

The memorial to John Ruskin in St Paul's Church, Herne Hill, unveiled on 8 February 1901, was designed by Brindley in the Venetian Byzantine style. The firm of Farmer & Brindley ceased business in 1929. In the 1930s the site of their workshops at 63 Westminster Bridge Road became part of Morley College.

## Thomas Lynn Bristowe (1833-92)
## 6 Herne Hill, 208 Herne Hill and 169 Denmark Hill
## Member of Parliament

Norwood's first Member of Parliament, Thomas Lynn Bristowe, was born in Camberwell 31 March 1833. He was one of seven children of a surgeon, John Syer Bristowe and his wife Mary.

Thomas was a member of the Stock Exchange firm of Bristowe Brothers, and from 1868 to 1885 a member of the Stock Exchange Committee. He was also for a time Captain of the No. 1 Company of the 1st Surrey Rifles, and Chairman of the Herne Hill and

Brixton Conservative Association. In the November 1885 general election he was elected Conservative MP for the newly created Norwood Division of Lambeth.

In 1888, the Lambeth Vestry and the Metropolitan Board of Works obtained consent to make a new public park on the east side of Brixton Hill, to be called Raleigh Park. When it became apparent that the Brockwell Estate would come on the market, Thomas Bristowe led a campaign to buy this larger and more attractive site. He took a Bill through Parliament to create the Park and led the committee to negotiate the price. He also helped raise the necessary funds by obtaining contributions from local authorities and the community. When there was some uncertainty as to whether enough would be raised, he personally guaranteed the money needed to ensure that the land for the park could be bought.

The formal opening, performed by Lord Rosebery, took place on 6 June 1892. However, at the end of the opening ceremony Thomas Bristowe collapsed on the steps of Brockwell Hall from a heart attack. Despite efforts to revive him, he died in the refreshment room. He was buried in Norwood Cemetery. In 1893 a drinking fountain was erected to his memory; until 1958 it stood near the Herne Hill entrance to Brockwell Park.

In the 1860s Thomas Bristowe was living on Herne Hill, where numbers 6 and 6A are today. From the mid 1860s to 1875 he lived at 208 Denmark Hill (demolished in the early 1900s), located between Sunset and Herne Hill Roads. From 1875 until 1885 he lived at Dulwich Hill House; by 1883 this was numbered 169 Denmark Hill. The house was demolished c1890; it occupied a site mid-way between Sunray Avenue and Red Post Hill. By the time of his death, Thomas had moved to a house in Kensington.

## Alice Burville (1856-1944)
## 221 Norwood Road
## Singer

Alice Julia Burville was born in Stepney 11 July 1856. Aged 18 she had her West End debut with the small part of Maid of Honour in a London production of the French operetta *La Branche Cassée* (The Broken Branch). She quickly rose to fame and the following year began a series of leading ingénue roles in a number of London productions. For the rest of the 1870s and the early 1880s she was one of the best known sopranos of her day. In 1877 she took over the role of Rosalinde in London's first *Die Fledermaus*; the following year she played Josephine in the first production of *HMS Pinafore*.

Alice toured America twice in a variety of roles: first in 1877 where she also sang in *HMS Pinafore*; then four years later in 1881 where, amongst other parts, she played Lady Angela in a

Broadway production of *Patience*. Alice returned to London and in 1882 appeared as Fiametta in the British production of Suppé's *Boccaccio*. However, this was to be her last major London appearance; thereafter she worked mainly in the provinces.

In 1876 Alice had married the actor and Savoy Opera singer William Henry Leigh Dugmore (1853-1915), whose stage name was W H Denny; but the marriage did not last. Her second husband was the composer and conductor John Crook, whom she may have met when playing the title role in *Merry Mignon*, one of his operettas. Her last known stage appearance was in Offenbach's *Geneviere de Brabant*, in Leicester in December 1893.

By 1918, Alice and her husband John were living at 221 Norwood Road. John died in 1922 and was buried in Norwood Cemetery. Alice stayed on at the house until 1924. She died in Littlehampton 4 July 1944, but is buried with her husband. Although she left £30 in her will for the upkeep in perpetuity of her and her husband's grave, the headstone has disappeared.

## James Callaghan (1912-2005) 7 Carver Road Prime Minister

The man known to his supporters as "Sunny Jim" lived at 7 Carver Road for a short while in 1967. After the Wilson Government's sterling devaluation, he resigned as Chancellor and immediately gave up his official residence at 11 Downing Street. George and Grace Thomson owned the house at 7 Carver Road, where they lived happily between 1963 and 1977. Since they were old friends of James Callaghan and his wife Audrey, the Thomsons lent them their house, moving temporarily to the Admiralty. When the Callaghans moved into their new home, a clutch of reporters came to Carver Road and interviewed a neighbour, Miss Hedges, who kept a

pristine house and was a pillar of both the Church and the Conservative Party. She became incandescent with rage on being asked whether she was a Labour Party supporter; her reply apparently echoed along the street. James Callaghan was collected by a large black chauffeur-driven official car each morning.

Leonard James Callaghan was brought up in poor circumstances in Portsmouth. His father was a naval Chief Petty Officer of Irish immigrant descent. James left Portsmouth Northern Secondary School at the age of 16 and became a tax clerk before serving in the Royal Navy in 1942. He married Audrey Moulton in 1938 and the couple had three children, one son and two daughters.

James Callaghan was first elected Labour MP for Cardiff South in 1945, serving under Clement Atlee as junior transport minister. He succeeded Harold Wilson as Prime Minister in 1976. However, during his time in office economic problems blighted the country, coming to a head in the winter of 1978-79 (the 'Winter of Discontent'). Callaghan lost a vote of no confidence in Parliament by one vote. As a result an election was called and he lost power to Margaret Thatcher in March 1979.

Callaghan remained in the House of Commons until 1987, retiring as a life peer and Knight of the Garter. He was the only Prime Minister who had held the other three great offices of state: Chancellor of the Exchequer (1964); Home Secretary (1967); Foreign Secretary (1974).

Despite his many political, social and economic problems, Callaghan gained respect and admiration among his colleagues. Margaret Thatcher described him as a "formidable opponent" and remembers him as having been "moved by a deep patriotism". Chancellor Gordon Brown said of him "while Jim rose to the top, he never forgot his roots".

James Callaghan died on 26 March 2005, the eve of his 93rd birthday, at his home in East Sussex. Just eleven days before, his wife had died aged 91. They were a devoted couple and had been married for 67 years.

## Mrs Patrick Campbell (1865-1940) 17 Milton Road Actress

Beatrice Rose Stella Tanner was born in Kensington 9 February 1865, the sixth and youngest child of John, son of an Anglo-Indian army accoutrement manufacturer, and Louisa (Maria Luigia Giovanna), daughter of Count Angelo Romanini, an Italian political exile. Stella had a peripatetic childhood and haphazard schooling as her father's fortunes rose and fell. At nine she moved to Tulse Dale Lodge, belonging to a friend of Louisa, between Tulse Hill and Dulwich; from 13 to 15 she lived at 14 Acacia Grove, Dulwich, owned by her uncle.

Stella studied piano at Guildhall School of Music and won a scholarship to Leipzig, but gave it up for love of tall, dark Patrick Campbell. He continually proposed; she accepted when she became pregnant, and they eloped 21 June 1884, lying about their ages. As the bank Patrick's father managed had failed, he took a poorly paid office job.

In late summer 1884 the couple took rooms at 17 Milton Road, Herne Hill. Their kind landlady, Mrs Charles Holder, promised them the large upstairs bedroom for Stella's

confinement at the same rent. When they could not pay that, she not only did not ask for the money, but lent them enough to buy food. At the end of December they moved to 8 Geneva Road, East Brixton, where their son was born in January. In 1886 they moved to Norwood, where a daughter was born.

Persuaded to join the Anomalies Dramatic Club of Norwood, Stella debuted 18 November 1886. Good reviews in *The Era* and *The Stage* encouraged her to go professional once she'd gained more experience. Patrick, meanwhile, emigrated to Brisbane, and later South Africa, to try to make money for the family. In October 1888, Stella made her professional debut in Liverpool as Mrs Patrick Campbell. After a successful run she returned to Acacia Grove, and subsequently toured as far as Dublin and Glasgow, and as near as Camberwell.

Soon she was to make her name as Rosalind in *As You Like It*, and in melodramas at the Adelphi. In 1893 she created the title role in Pinero's *The Second Mrs Tanqueray*, a career high point. From 1895-98 she was in partnership with actor-manager Forbes-Robinson, then formed her own company, on tour and at the Royalty. In April 1900, her husband was killed in the Boer War.

In 1901 she undertook the first of several American tours; and in subsequent years she starred in plays by Ibsen, Yeats and Sardou. On 6 April 1914 she married George Cornwallis-West, days before she opened in Shaw's *Pygmalion*. Her friendship and correspondence with G B Shaw lasted many years. Cornwallis-West, however, deserted her in December 1919, leaving huge debts. Her London stage career continued until 1929; she then made a few films in Hollywood. She spent her last months in France, where she died on 9 April 1940.

## Sidney Carter (1915-2004)
## 39 Holmdene Avenue
## Poet, Folk Musician and Songwriter

Sydney Bertram Carter was born 6 May 1915 and died 1 March 2004. He lived at 39 Holmdene Avenue for 35 years until his death. He was born in Camden Town, attended school in Islington and at Christ's Hospital, Horsham, Surrey. He read History at Balliol College, Oxford, where he started to write poetry. After graduating he taught at Frensham Heights School, Farnham.

Sydney's abhorrence of violence led him to serve in the Friends Ambulance Unit in WW2, in the Middle East and Greece. He identified with the Friends' reliance on personal experience, social activism and their affirmation of God's presence in every human being.

After the War Sydney worked for the British Council, resettling refugees in England and teaching in mainland Europe. In 1955 he married Natalia Beckendorff, a Rumanian émigrée. However, she died in a climbing accident shortly afterwards.

His interest in folk music was influenced by A L Lloyd, the folk song collector, and the music he had heard in Greece. Folk music became a consuming part of his life. In 1952 he began to write lyrics for Donald Swann's reviews; also he and Sheila Hancock collaborated in an LP album *Putting Out the Dustbin*. This included the song 'The Last Cigarette', which became a mini classic. He also wrote the CND marching song 'I Want a Little Bomb Like You'; and six songs on Donald Swann's EP *Songs of Faith and Doubt*. He also worked as a critic on the *Gramophone*.

Sydney's greatest successes were the songs 'Lord of the Dance', which provided the theme for Michael Flatley's show of the same name, and 'One More Step'. Both songs are very popular in school assemblies.

Many of Sydney's songs were on the theme of belief and doubt. He once said that he "saw Christ in the incarnation of the piper who is calling us to sing of the dancing pattern of life". Two books *The Rock of Doubt* (1978) and *Dance in the Dark* (1980) set out the signposts of his journey through the holiness of humanity.

In his last years Sydney was devotedly cared for by his wife Leela Nour. After his death, their son Michael gave a moving tribute to his father in a *Songs of Praise* television programme. Sydney was cremated at Norwood Cemetery.

## David Chadwick (1821-95)
## 6 Herne Hill
## Accountant and Company Promoter

Born 23 December 1821 at Macclesfield in Cheshire, David Chadwick was the youngest of nine children. He had little formal schooling; however, by attending evening classes he was able to follow his father into accountancy, setting up his own practice in 1843. In 1844 he married Louisa; the couple had a son and two daughters.

David was appointed Treasurer to the Corporation of Salford, the town's gasworks as well as the waterworks and magistrates. He published many papers and pamphlets on sanitary and educational issues, frequently combining his interest in statistics with the investigation of urban problems and conditions. A council member of the Statistical Society of London from 1865 to 1867, he was also President of the Manchester Statistical Society.

Between 1860 and 1892 David had ten business associates, from seven of whom he was separated by lawsuits.

Nevertheless his practice prospered, and between 1862 and 1874 he was responsible for transforming at least 47 companies from private partnerships to public ownership. By the 1870s his activities encompassed domestic and American railway shares and bonds, American land sales, shares in overseas mining, telegraph, utility and tramway companies.

David's national importance as an industrial financier resulted in his being called to give expert evidence before various Parliamentary Committees. In 1868 he was elected as the Liberal MP for Macclesfield, but he was unseated twelve years later following allegations of bribery and other electoral malpractice.

David Chadwick played an important role in professionalising accountancy. He was a founder member and Fellow of the Institute of Accountants and the first President of the Manchester Institute of Chartered Accountants. In 1881 he became one of the first council members of the Institute of Chartered Accountants in England and Wales, a position he held until his death. He was also involved with establishing Royal Holloway College, later becoming a Governor.

Louisa Chadwick died in 1877, some two years after they had moved to The Poplars on Herne Hill. A year later David married Ursula (d 1900), daughter of the eminent mining engineer Thomas Sopwith, and aunt of the famous aeroplane designer.

Her increasingly self-opinionated husband had dramatic public clashes with the boards of the companies he had promoted. An obituary writer later said that he had an "aversion to criticism, advice or opposition, or even to listen to caution".

The 1880s saw a decline of his entrepreneurial energy, although he continued to work as an accountant and to write and publish occasional pamphlets on economic and financial matters. However, apart from billiards, he had no hobbies or other interests. In later years he suffered from impaired vision and increasing deafness, which must have made his company even more difficult to bear. David died at his home, The Poplars, on 19 September 1895, survived by his second wife. He was buried in Norwood Cemetery.

The Poplars was demolished c1910. It was located on the site of the present numbers 6 and 6A Herne Hill.

## Richard Church (1893-1972)
## 2 Warmington Road
## Poet and Novelist

Born in Battersea 26 March 1893, Richard Thomas Church was the second son of Tom, a postman at South West District, and Lavinia Orton Church, elementary school teacher at Horseferry Road SW1. Lavinia later transferred to a London Board school in Battersea Park Road, "even more rough" than the Surrey Lane Higher Grade School Richard and brother Jack (1889-1927) attended.

In winter 1904-05 the family sought a healthier district to cure Lavinia's bronchial asthma. They found Goldencourt, now 2 Warmington Road, "a unique house .... at the post-barred

end of a lane ... called Ruskin Walk." Fifty years later, Richard wrote with renewed boyhood excitement: "A row of aspens ran ... to the top of the hill," beyond which "a few acres of meadow land, with a real hedge and derelict farm buildings, stretched as far as Herne Hill station. An old horse brooded by a pond ... it was half-way to paradise." They moved into the detached, double-fronted £550 house on 25 March 1905. It had been built by the architect of Kennington Theatre for his own use, with lavish gold lincrusta in "bold oriental splendour", Alma Tadema fireplace and floor to ceiling mirrors in the drawing room. In his attic room, Richard woke to thrushes and blackbirds singing in the great elms across Half Moon Lane.

At Dulwich Hamlet School he excelled in the arts and English. He drew and painted with passion and loved reading, a chief discovery being John Ruskin. In 1908 Richard won a scholarship to Camberwell Art School; however, his father insisted he earn a living. Though hating the prospect of becoming a civil servant, he took evening classes for the boy clerk's exam, while nursing his mother during the day. In April 1909 he started work at the Land Registry. Having given up art, Richard began writing as a means of self-expression. His first verses were accepted by the *Clarion*, whose editor said the young author "should go far."

His mother's death in April 1910 shattered him. With the fence removed and the aspens being felled to widen Ruskin Walk, the funeral procession was the first traffic round the house into Half Moon Lane.

One year later he was a permanent civil servant at Customs House. When their father remarried, Richard and Jack sought their own place, taking rooms off Dog Kennel Hill. Jack married in 1913 and moved to Camberwell. In 1916 Richard married his step-sister, Caroline Jessica Parfett. Rejected for WWl service by army doctors, he moved with his bride that September to Lipsfield, Kent. They had a daughter, but later divorced. In 1930 he married Catherina Anna Schemmer; they had three children. Catherina died in 1965 and two years later he married Dorothy Mary Beale.

While continuing to work in the Government Laboratory and later the Ministry of Labour, Richard became a successful writer, well known long before he left the Civil Service in 1933. From 1917 onwards he published 21 volumes of poetry, a verse play, 17 novels, 16 non-fiction works and a three-volume autobiography. He was awarded the Femina Vie Heureuse

Prize, Foyle Poetry Prize and the Sunday Times Gold Medal. An established editor, literary critic, essayist and lecturer, he was Director of the English Festival of Spoken Verse, President of PEN and of The English Association. A vice-president and Fellow of the Royal Society of Literature and vice-president of the Royal Literary Fund, he was awarded the CBE in 1957.

Richard Church died at Sissinghurst 4 March 1972. Subsequently, Southwark Council placed a plaque on 2 Warmington Road, his "magic home in a magic land".

## Joe Clark (1868-1940)
## 31 and 32 Ferndene Road
## Master Plasterer

Joseph Bernard Clark was born 25 March 1868 in Dundee, the eldest of ten children. Following in his father's footsteps, he learned the trade of decorative plastering. However, a slump in the building industry forced the family to leave Scotland for London to seek work.

In 1913, Joe Clark, together with Harry Fenn, a surveyor, founded the firm of Clark & Fenn based at Loughborough Junction, but later moving to Clapham Old Town and then to Mitcham. Clark & Fenn really made its name with the development of cinemas and theatres, where extensive use was made of decorative plasterwork. They made complicated and ornamental shapes with fibrous plaster, i.e. gypsum plaster cast into gelatine or plaster moulds and reinforced with coarse canvas. This technique has the advantage of off-site manufacture, work being produced to the required design in manageable sections. These could then be transported complete and dry and assembled on the site.

Clark & Fenn's prestigious theatre contracts included restoring and decorating the Theatre Royal Drury Lane, the Grand Theatre at Leeds, the London Palladium and the Queen's Theatre and Royal Court in London. They also carried out work at Somerset House in the Strand, the Plaisterers' Hall in the City of London, Hertford House off Oxford Street (home of the Wallace Collection), St Clement Danes Church in the Strand and the Granada Cinema at Tooting.

In 1892, Joe married Mary Brown at St John's Church, Hammersmith; and from 1893-1915 they lived in Fulham. From 1903-09 he served as Alderman on Fulham Borough Council. Around 1919 the family moved to 31 Ferndene Road, Herne Hill. Joe bought a plot of land in Ferndene Road overlooking Ruskin Park. Here in 1924 he built a substantial detached villa for himself, now 32 Ferndene Road, introducing his decorative plasterwork to the domestic scene. He had already joined the

Ruskin Park Bowling Club, moving a few years later to the Temple Bowling Club in Sunset Road, where he became Vice-Chairman and President.

Joe Clark died 1 February 1940 at Hove and is buried at Norwood Cemetery. Clark & Fenn Ltd. are still in business in Mitcham. In 1976 the firm was taken over by Trafalgar House, who in turn were taken over in 1996 by Kvaerner.

## Rev. George Clayton (1783-1862) 20 Herne Hill Congregational Minister

George Clayton was the second son of Rev. John Clayton (1754-1843), the pastor of King's Weighhouse Independent Chapel, Fish Street Hill in the City of London. He trained for the ministry at Reading and at Hoxton Academy and in 1802, aged 19, was appointed a co-pastor at Southampton. His next appointment, to York Street Chapel, Walworth in 1804, was to last 51 years; and his ministry was to make a great impact on the local community.

First known as Lock's Fields Chapel, York Street Chapel was built in 1790 and had been without a minister for a number of years. George Clayton came to an area that had just changed from being a country village to a growing middle-class London suburb.

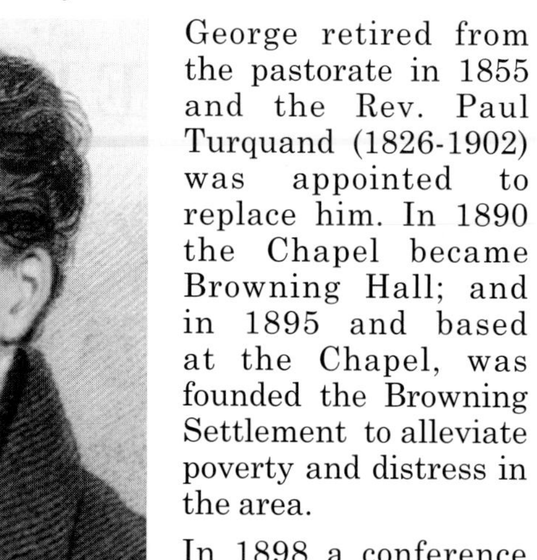

Well-known names that came to worship at York Street Chapel included Capt. James Wilson and Robert Moffat (1795-1883), missionary and father-in-law to David Livingstone. In 1812, George christened the infant Robert Browning (1812-89), whose parents lived at Rainbow Cottage, Cottage Green off Southampton Way in Camberwell, and in 1821, the infant Henry Doulton (1820-97) the Lambeth potter. Robert Browning, with his family, attended regularly at the Chapel until he was 16. When young, he was reprimanded from the pulpit by George Clayton "for restlessness and inattention".

In the 1810s George lived at Canterbury Place, Walworth and in the mid 1830s at Manor Place, also in Walworth. However, for a number of years in the late 1820s/early 1830s and again in the late 1840s, he lived at 20 Herne Hill. The house was later demolished, but occupied a site now opposite Casino Avenue and next to Dorchester Court.

In 1854, on the 50th anniversary of his ministry, a school for 750 pupils was started next to the Chapel and named the Clayton Memorial School.

George retired from the pastorate in 1855 and the Rev. Paul Turquand (1826-1902) was appointed to replace him. In 1890 the Chapel became Browning Hall; and in 1895 and based at the Chapel, was founded the Browning Settlement to alleviate poverty and distress in the area.

In 1898 a conference held there by the social reformer, Charles Booth (1840-1916) started the campaign which culminated in the Old Age Pension Act of 1908. York Street became Browning Street in 1921.

In 1804 George married Mary Whennel (d 1842) and in 1845, Rebecca Mary Giles (d 1874) of Clapham Common. He died on 14 July 1862 at Gaines (or Gaynes) Villa, Upminster in Essex and is buried in Abney Park Cemetery, Stoke Newington.

### Father Peter Clements (1921-99) St Philip & St James, Poplar Walk Parish Priest

Born in Hastings, Father Peter was ordained to the priesthood in May 1947 and worked as assistant priest in several parishes: Deal, Dartford, Rotherhithe, Eastbourne and Caterham. He became the first parish priest of Our Lady of the Assumption, Tooting in 1963, transferring to St Philip and St James, Herne Hill ten years later. He was much loved by his parishioners, serving them faithfully until poor health forced his retirement in 1986. Father Peter celebrated his golden jubilee as a priest in 1997, and remained a true friend to the community until his death in August 1999.

Father Peter was a supporter and founder member of the Herne Hill Society and served on the Committee. He offered the use of his church hall for the Society's inaugural meeting and for regular monthly meetings that were held there from 1982-92. He is buried in Norwood Cemetery.

### Howard Colls (1846-1910) 2 Grove Place Builder

John Howard Colls was born in Camberwell 30 August 1846. His father, Benjamin, was a successful housepainter and builder with a business based at 240-246 Camberwell Road. Working for his father, Howard acquired his practical building skills. In 1867 he married a shipbuilder's daughter Annie McMillan; they had one son and at least seven daughters. In 1878 Benjamin died and the business passed to Howard and his older brother William Abraham Colls (1842-93). Under their joint management, Colls and Sons expanded, specialising in building City offices and banks, and achieving a sound reputation for craftsmanship and quality.

Howard Colls was vice-president of the National Association of Master Builders of Great Britain (1885-89) and President (1889-90). Whilst President of the Institute of Builders, from 1887 to 1888, he was mainly instrumental in drawing up a standard form of contract between builder and architect, still in use today.

He was also heavily involved in the 'eight-hour-day' dispute with the London United Trade Committee of Carpenters and Joiners. This dispute, with strikes and lock-outs, was particularly hard fought, and for much

of 1891 brought building in London to a virtual standstill. It was eventually settled with hours of work being reduced and overtime rates being increased.

After his brother's death in 1893, Howard became involved in a four year legal battle with the Home and Colonial Stores over the definition of 'ancient lights'. Home and Colonial objected to his building a warehouse opposite their offices that they said would spoil their view. This fight went all the way to the House of Lords who, in 1904, ruled that the Home and Colonial Stores was entitled to sufficient air and light for ordinary purposes, but did not have a perpetual right to the same amount as they had previously enjoyed. This represented a significant modification of the law that still applies today.

In 1903, Colls and Sons merged with George Trollope and Sons, to form Trollope and Colls. Howard Colls and George Trollope were joint Chairmen. The new company was very successful and expanded into other areas such as fitting out ocean liners. The Trollope and the Colls families retained their involvement with the company into the 1960s, when it was bought by Trafalgar House Investments in 1968. It was later absorbed into the Swedish Skanska Group becoming Skanska UK.

For a time during the 1860s Howard Colls lived at 2 Grove Place (later 127 Denmark Hill). Grove Place was a terrace of nine houses behind the former Fox-under-the-Hill public house, located on the south corner of Champion Park. The houses were bombed in WW2 and subsequently demolished. He died at or near Buenos Aires on 29 December 1910, suffering a heart attack while on a sea cruise for the sake of his health.

## John Dibblee Crace (1838-1919)
## Springfield, Half Moon Lane
## Interior Decorator and Designer

John Dibblee Crace was born 19 January 1838 at 14 (later 38) Wigmore Street, London. He was the eldest of eleven surviving children of John Gregory Crace and his wife Sarah Jane Hine Langley. John Gregory ran the successful firm of Crace, designers and decorators, that had been founded by his great-grandfather Edward. In c1859 the entire Crace family moved to Springfield in Half Moon Lane, a large Italianate house (now demolished) with a land frontage stretching from the Half Moon Tavern to Burbage Road.

John Dibblee Crace showed his artistic gifts at an early age. After schooling in Tunbridge Wells, he was apprenticed to his grandfather, Frederick Crace, who was decorating the Royal Pavilion, Brighton. John Dibblee's formal education ended at age 17, when John Gregory suffered a partial breakdown.

The father's ill health meant that he had to take on all the firm's current commissions, though he was helped by his grandfather, Frederick, who came out of retirement. Despite these responsibilities, he continued with his studies, particularly of Italian and European decorative art in which he maintained an interest for the rest of his life. He also had a fascination for Islamic Art, no doubt stimulated by a visit, in 1868-69, to Egypt and Palestine.

In 1873 John Dibblee became a full partner in the Crace firm and married Caroline Elizabeth Foster (1845-1947). They had eleven children. At about this time he was working on two important commissions: Knightshayes Court, Devon and the Pompeian Room at Ickworth House, Suffolk, both in conjunction with architect Francis Penrose. However, the highlight of his career was the series of state and private rooms in Renaissance style at Longleat House (1875-77) for the 4th Marquis of Bath. In April 1885, the French Emperor Napoleon III and Princess Eugenie paid a State visit to Britain; and the Crace firm was commissioned to decorate rooms at Windsor Castle for their reception. Other major commissions included re-decorating Leeds Town Hall (1892) and the Royal Pavilion, Brighton (1894). They also included Cliveden House, Grosvenor House and Burlington House. His 1887 ceiling in the main staircase hall of The National Gallery in Trafalgar Square was recently restored after being over-painted in white during WW2.

In 1899, when he was 61, John Dibblee decided to close the family firm. He said this was because he had no partner with whom to share the burden of running the business; and he did not want the problems created by trade union action and the Employers Liability Acts. He lectured on art subjects, published numerous articles and two books, notably *The Art of Colour Decoration* (1912).

John Dibblee Crace died on 19 November 1919 and was buried in Norwood Cemetery.

The Victoria and Albert Museum and the Royal Institute of British Architects together hold the family archives and a large collection of Crace drawings. Future generations will thus continue to have access to the work of this remarkable family.

## John Gregory Crace (1808-89)
## Springfield, Half Moon Lane
## Interior Decorator and Designer

For 131 years the Crace family ran what was, by virtue of the number and importance of its commissions, this country's most important firm of decorators. The company, founded in 1768, prospered under the unbroken management of five generations of Craces, until it ceased operation in 1899.

John Gregory Crace was born 26 May 1808 at 24 Curzon Street. He was the elder of two surviving sons of Frederick Crace (1779-1859) and his wife Augusta Harrop Gregory (c1783-1827). He was educated at Dr Crombie's school in Greenwich and later at Pollard's school, South Kensington.

John Gregory began his career apprenticed to his father, working on Worcester House and Buckingham Palace. In 1830, a legacy from his mother's estate enabled him to become a full partner in his father's business, rather fortuitous as his father was owed money by King George IV. He travelled extensively round Europe, seeking inspiration and ideas that he put into practice on his return.

On 26 January 1833, John Gregory married Sarah Jane Hine (1815-94). They had 13 children. The firm prospered and their many commissions included work at Knebworth House, Abney Hall, the Palace of Westminster and Chatsworth House in Derbyshire, where he created a remarkable library in the 'old French style' for the 6th Duke of Devonshire. For some eight years from 1844 he collaborated with the architect A W Pugin. Amongst their collaborative efforts was the care and conservation of an important collection of early textiles at Haddon Hall, Derbyshire. From 1880-82, Crace worked on the Waterloo Room at Windsor Castle.

John Gregory achieved wider fame through his work for the international exhibitions in London, Paris and Manchester between 1851 and 1862. As a result, he received still further civic and international commissions. He published articles on colour theory, decorative practices and the first history of wallpaper and in 1862 became a founder member of the Photographic Society.

In c1859 the Crace family moved to Springfield in Half Moon Lane. Now demolished, the house's name survives in the Springfield Estate. John Gregory died on 13 August 1889. He is buried in Norwood Cemetery along with his father Frederick and son John Dibblee Crace.

## John Francis Crook (1847-1922)
## 221 Norwood Road
## Composer and Conductor

John Francis Crook was born in Marylebone in 1847. He is said to have had piano lessons from his aunt, Madame de Belleville Oury, a pupil of Beethoven. He went to Norwich where he studied harmony and counterpoint, and was appointed organist at St John's Catholic Chapel.

John became a conductor, making his base in Manchester. He performed there and toured around the North West with a variety of musical productions. He also became a prolific songwriter, achieving national and international success for his musical comedies and his music hall Cockney songs. He supplied songs for many of the day's top performers - most famously 'The Coster's Serenade' for Albert Chevalier. His original 1905 score for J M Barrie's *Peter Pan* is still performed today.

In the 1890s John moved to London where his career as a conductor and composer continued to prosper. He worked regularly for many leading theatres including the Prince of Wales, the Theatre Royal Drury Lane, the Adelphi (1895-98), the Lyceum, the Duke of York's and the Vaudeville (1901).

John was married to the soprano, Alice Burville. From 1918 they lived at 221 Norwood Road until his death on 10 November 1922. He is buried with his wife in Norwood Cemetery; but their monument has disappeared.

## Brass Crosby (1725-1793)
## 68 Half Moon Lane
## Lawyer and Politician

Brass Crosby got his unusual forename through his mother, the daughter of John Brass, a local worthy in Stockton-on-Tees, where Brass was born 8 May 1725. He was the eldest son of the five children of Hercules and Mary Crosby.

After serving a legal apprenticeship in Sunderland, Brass came to London and set up as an attorney. His parents followed him, settling in Stoke Newington, Hercules having squandered his wife's money on an ill-fated coal mining project.

Brass married three times, each time to a wealthy widow - Sarah Walraven (in 1748) with whom he had one daughter; Mrs Cook, widow of a collar-maker to the ordnance; and finally in 1772 Mary, widow of John Tattersall, Rector of Gatton, and daughter of James Maud, London wine merchant. Mary brought him a large fortune of some £25,000 as well as the manor of Chelsfield near Orpington, Kent.

Brass began his political career in 1758 as a member of the Common Council for Tower Ward. Thereafter he held a succession of City offices including that of Remembrancer, which he bought for £3,600 in 1760 and sold the following year. He went on to serve as Sheriff (1764-65), and in February 1765 was elected Alderman. Three years later he bought his way into national politics, being elected MP for Honiton, a notoriously 'venal borough'.

In 1770 Brass was elected Lord Mayor and immediately declared that, at the risk of his life, he would protect the "just privileges and liberties" of the City of London. One of his first acts was to refuse to back Admiralty warrants

for press-ganging men into naval service, ordering constables to be positioned "at all avenues" of the City to prevent men being seized.

The following year Brass gained greater celebrity for his role in the 'Printers' Case'. John Wheble and Roger Thompson had been arrested for printing reports of parliamentary debates, then a breach of privilege. They were discharged when they appeared before the City magistrates. When another printer, John Miller of the *London Evening Post*, was summoned to appear before the House, the messenger bringing the summons was arrested. Brass refused to release him and was ordered to attend the Commons. He defended himself by arguing that he was bound by his Aldermanic oath to protect the rights of the City. Despite being supported by an enormous disorderly crowd, Brass was committed to the Tower of London. Several judges refused to hear the case against him, and he was released at the end of the parliamentary session. He returned in triumph to the Mansion House, having successfully defied the Commons and indirectly secured the right to report parliamentary debates. With a valuable cup, the Corporation thanked him for supporting "the liberties of the Corporation, and for having defended the constitution". This encounter with the House of Commons is the origin of the saying, "as bold as brass".

Despite failing to secure a Parliamentary seat in elections in 1774 and 1784, Brass continued to accumulate offices - President of the Bethlem and Bridewell Hospital (1782) and Governor of the Irish Society (1783). At the time of his death after a short illness on 14 February 1793 at his house in Chatham Place, Blackfriars Bridge, he was still Chair of four City committees. He was buried in the churchyard at Chelsfield, Kent.

In 1771, an obelisk was erected to Brass in the centre of St George's Circus, when it was laid out along with Blackfriars Road. The obelisk was moved in 1905 to a position outside Bethlem Hospital (now the Imperial War Museum) but in 2002 was restored to its original site in St George's Circus.

From 1756 until about 1775, Brass Crosby lived in Dulwich Place, a house set in some 16 acres almost exactly on the site of the present King's College Botanical Department at 68 Half Moon Lane.

After his marriage to Mary Tattersall, he left Herne Hill to live in Chelsfield Lodge, his and Mary's main residence for the last 22 years of his life.

## Robert James Culverwell (1802-52)
## 3 Grove Place
## Physician

Robert Culverwell was born 13 July 1802. He studied medicine in London and qualified as an apothecary in 1824. The following year he set up a medical practice in north London. Although working "amongst the labouring poor", as described in his 1855 autobiography, the practice prospered and expanded. But being ambitious, Robert looked for other ways to make his fortune. He wrote a great many popular books and pamphlets on a variety of medical subjects. His *Guide to Health and Long Life* (1844) describes the benefits of a proper, balanced and moderate diet and the effects on youth of succumbing to the temptations of "smoking, drinking, late hours and licentiousness". Other publications included *Domestic Handbook for Invalids* (1842) and *How to Live 100 years* (1848).

Robert had a particular interest in bathing and its use for treating conditions such as gout, fever and leprosy. Putting his theories into practice, he opened a bathing establishment in the City, close to the Bank of England, where he offered treatments based on warm, cold, medicated and sulphur baths, as well as shampooing. His business thrived, but he took on too many liabilities and got into financial difficulties. After paying off his debts, he opened premises in New Bond Street, but without much success, and was forced to move to Gravesend.

Still undeterred, he tried once again with a new bathing establishment in New Bond Street, later moving to the Strand. Finally, in 1852, Robert opened premises at what was then 10 Argyll Place, on the site of the present London Palladium, opposite Liberty's. Here he seems to have done well, for his household then ran to seven employees. However, he died the same year and was buried in Norwood Cemetery.

Robert Culverwell spent much of his life on the move. However, in the 1840s, he was living at 3 Grove Place. Grove Place no longer exists; the houses there were bombed in WW2 and subsequently demolished. It was a short street off Champion Hill, running parallel to Denmark Hill, approximately where the block of flats, Allport House, is today.

## Joseph James Curling (1844-1906)
## 36 Herne Hill
## Soldier, Priest and Yachtsman

Born at 36 Herne Hill (The Quadrangle was built on the site in 1911), former home of William Leaf, Joseph James Curling was the only child of Joseph Curling (1798-1866), furniture printer, and Charlotte Holbert Curling (1807-57), youngest daughter of Captain James Wilson. After education at Harrow School and The Royal Military Academy at Woolwich, he served in the army from 1865-73, including postings as ADC to the Governor of Bermuda (1868-69) and ADC to the Inspector-General of Fortifications (1869-73).

Joseph left the army to enter the priesthood, serving as a missionary in the Bay of Islands, and then as Rural Dean of the Strait of Belle Isle, both in Newfoundland (then independent of Canada). Later in life he entered Oriel College, Oxford, obtaining an MA in theology in 1890. From 1891-92 he was Principal of the Theological College at St Johns, Newfoundland. On returning to England, Joseph served as vicar of Hamble-le-Rice near Southampton (1892-1900). In 1904 he became vice-president of the Society for the Propagation of the Gospel in Foreign Parts.

One of his many recreations was sailing. In 1882 he received his

certificate as yacht-master from the Board of Trade. He gave his yacht, Lavrock, a yawl of 72 tons, to Dr Field, Bishop of Newfoundland after skippering her from Portsmouth to St Johns.

Joseph lived through two near-death experiences. The first was in the Blackheath Railway Tunnel crash of 1864 when he survived to help the injured. The second, in 1902, was caused by a fall from his horse while riding in Rotten Row, Hyde Park. He died 18 February 1906 at his home, Denholme, Datchet, Buckinghamshire, leaving a wife, three sons and a daughter and £107,017 in his will.

## Charles Druce (1792-1881)
## 168 Denmark Hill
## Solicitor

Charles Druce practised as a solicitor throughout his working life and became head of the firm of Druce, Sons and Jackson, a large mercantile law practice. At the time of his death he was one of the oldest practising solicitors in London. Charles entered the firm in 1814 and worked for 66 years in their offices at 10 Billiter Square. At first he was in partnership with his father, Charles Druce (1760-1845), and brother, John Druce (c1800-69); and later with his sons, Charles Claridge Druce (1819-85) and Alexander Devas Druce (c1827-97). Charles also served as clerk to the Inn Holders' Company and as solicitor to the Dulwich College Estate.

Charles was born 28 March 1792. About 1804 his father moved home from the City of London to Dulwich, so Charles spent some of his childhood there. In 1818 he married Ann Claridge (1797-1874), the daughter of John Fellowes Claridge of Sevenoaks. Over the next 25 years the couple had 18 children - eight sons and ten daughters. About 1835 the family moved to 168 Denmark Hill, one of the largest detached houses in the locality, formerly inhabited by Samuel Sanders and later known as Dane House. At the time of the 1841 census, there were 19 people at home including ten children and six servants. The house was demolished c1906. The lake in Ruskin Park used to be in the Druce's back garden.

In his later years Charles served as President of the Camberwell Dispensary (see Otto August Benecke); his name still remains on the plaque at 325 Camberwell New Road. At his death on 10 January 1881, at least five of his by now middle-aged children were still living at home. They later moved to a smaller property at 198 Denmark Hill (on the site of what is now part of Deepdene Road). Charles Druce and some of his family are buried at Norwood Cemetery.

### George Druce (1821-69)
### 168 Denmark Hill
### Barrister

The second son of Charles Druce, George Druce was born 22 February 1821. Educated at Shrewsbury School and at St Peter's College, Cambridge, he trained as a barrister. He was called to the bar in 1846 at Lincoln's Inn, and appointed Queen's Counsel in 1866. He died in a riding accident on 15 April 1869, aged only 48.

George had a brilliant legal career as a junior barrister, showing great promise. His reputation had grown steadily and he had proved to be a formidable rival to the leading court advocates of the time. His legal expertise and knowledge was considerable and he was noted for his mastery of facts and the clearness and precision of his arguments. He never married and is buried in his father's grave at Norwood Cemetery.

### Norman Druce (1875-1954)
### 163 Denmark Hill
### Cricketer

Norman Frank Druce was the grandson of Charles Druce. His father, Walter Druce (1833-1905), a distiller, moved into 163 Denmark Hill in 1871 soon after the previous owner, John Ruskin, had left for his new home in the Lake District. Norman was born and brought up at 163 Denmark Hill.

Norman was educated at Marlborough School and Trinity College, Cambridge. While at Cambridge he excelled at cricket, obtaining his blue when a freshman, as a middle-order, right-handed batsman. He played against Oxford at Lord's in each of his four years (1894-97). In his final year he was Captain, and the team won by 179 runs. His highest score for Oxford was 72 runs in 1896. In 1895 Norman was selected to represent the Gentlemen against the Players at Lord's, where he played a stylish innings of 50 runs. He made seven centuries for the University including 199 not out against the MCC, and had the highest Cambridge batting averages in 1895 (56) and 1897 (66). As an amateur he played twelve matches for Surrey County Cricket Club, and in 1897-98 he went on tour to Australia with A E Stoddart's MCC team, playing 30 innings with an average of 34 runs.

On his return from Australia, Norman gave up first-class cricket and entered his father's distillery business, J S Smith, Druce and Co. Ltd, of Cephas Street, Mile End Road. His father died in 1905 leaving £203,624 in his will. In 1908 the distillery business was wound up, and at the age of 33 Norman retired. He died 27 October 1954 aged 79 in a hotel at Milford-on-Sea, Hampshire and left £73,423 in his will. His eldest brother, George Druce (1872-1963), also played cricket for Cambridge University.

### Henry Havelock Ellis (1859-1939)
### 24 Holmdene Avenue
### Writer and Sexologist

The only son of Edward Pepper Ellis and Susannah Mary (née Wheatley) was born in Croydon 2 February 1859. His father and maternal grandfather were sea captains; Henry was named after the latter's cousin, Sir Henry Havelock, an army General who served

during the Indian Mutiny. At seven he voyaged around the world; at 16 he sailed to Australia, remaining four years. He later studied medicine at St Thomas's Hospital, London, gaining a license with the Society of Apothecaries.

In 1883 he joined a socialist debating group which became the Fabian Society. Associates included Annie Bessant, G B Shaw, Edward Carpenter, Walter Crane and H G Wells. He also wrote for monthly reviews and edited the 'Mermaid' series on Elizabethan and Jacobean dramatists, and the 'Contemporary Science' series, both of which made their subjects widely accessible.

A supporter of sexual liberation, Ellis formed romantic attachments with several women, notably Olive Schreiner, author of *The Story of an African Farm*, and writer-lecturer Edith Mary Oldham Lees, whom he married in 1891. She shared his love of freedom and experiment; living together in Cornwall and elsewhere, she impulsively spent the little money they had. Edith died in 1916.

Ellis wrote *The New Spirit* (1890) and *Man and Woman* (1894). His six-volume *Studies in the Psychology of Sex* appeared from 1897-1910, causing controversy; *Sexual Inversion* was prosecuted in 1898. Banned in Britain, the books were published in the US and translated into many languages. Later works include *The Erotic Rights of Women* (1918), the play, *Function of Sex* (1921) and *Little Essays of Love and Virtue* (1922). In 1928 he added a seventh volume to the *Studies*.

His close friend Margaret Sanger, leader of the world birth control movement, gave Ellis a special 70th birthday present. She proposed that his companion, Françoise Lafitte Cyon, give up her teaching job; Margaret would pay the equivalent of her salary so she could act as his secretary and they could live together. They found 24 Holmdene Avenue, which Françoise christened 'Fairy Tale House'. Ellis said it ought to be called 'House of the *Dance of Life'* since the American sale of that book helped pay for it. Françoise left her East End home, bringing her two sons; and Ellis left his flat in Canterbury Crescent, Brixton, where he had lived 20 years. They moved to Herne Hill in May 1929, joined by housekeeper Bessie Girling.

Ellis spent a third of his time there, writing and revising in self-contained upstairs rooms. Writers and admirers from around the world visited him; those seeking help and encouragement included Radclyffe Hall. He also stayed at Haslemere Cottage in

Wivelsfield Green, Sussex, which Margaret took on long lease. He kept typescripts of his autobiography in both locations.

After Bessie fell ill and Henry suffered from pleurisy, it was decided to leave both house and cottage. In 1938 Henry and Françoise moved to a small house at Hentlesham, Suffolk; he died there 8 July 1939. His autobiography, *My Life*, was published in 1940.

## Richard Whitemen Fall (1821-78)
## 44 Herne Hill
## Boyhood Friend of John Ruskin

In the 1820s the Falls moved from Walworth to 44 Herne Hill, near to the Ruskins at number 28. The parents, Richard (1790-1863), a Customs official, and Eliza (1799-1849), had two children. In his early years their only son, Richard Whiteman Fall, was a close friend of John Ruskin, often spending time in Ruskin's top floor room, reading or writing. They also enjoyed taking their dogs for walks together. However, from 1834-37 when Fall was away at Shrewsbury School, he saw Ruskin only during school holidays.

In 1841 the young Fall accompanied Ruskin on a trip to Wales, Ruskin's first holiday without his parents. Later, in 1849, they toured the Alps together. The two friends gradually lost touch with each other. Unlike Ruskin, Fall led a conventional life: he married, had three children and worked in a merchant's office. By 1856 he was living at 115 Denmark Hill (the site is now part of the Maudsley Hospital) and by 1860 at a large mansion (now gone) he called Severn House at 77 Thornton Road, Clapham Park. He died 18 March 1878 and is buried in Norwood Cemetery.

Fall's boyhood home at 44 Herne Hill (later called Glanpaith, demolished in the 1890s) was located opposite Holmdene Avenue on the site of the present 50 and 52 Herne Hill.

Fall's sister Eliza (1822-81) never married and lived with her parents. She was a firm friend of Ruskin's mother, Margaret, spending much time with her after Ruskin's father died in 1864. John Ruskin described Eliza as "an entirely worthy and unworldly girl" and on another occasion as "brilliant at a Christmas party". For a time from about 1870, Eliza lived with her brother at Clapham Park, and later at 11 George Street, Hanover Square. She died 17 August 1881 at Great Malvern, Worcestershire.

## Rotimi Fani-Kayode (1955-89)
## 151 Railton Road
## Artist and Photographer

Rotimi, son of Remi, Balogun of Ife, was born in Lagos, Nigeria, 20 April 1955. The aristocratic Kayode family were keepers of the Shrine of Yoruba deities and priests of Ifa, the oracular spirit. Aged 11 when the 1966 coup led to the Nigerian Civil War, Rotimi left for England. After nine years in Gloucestershire and Somerset, he went on to take an economics degree at Georgetown University, Washington DC, and an MA in Fine Art at the Pratt Institute, New York. Returning to London in 1983, he lived and worked at 151 Railton Road, establishing himself as a photographer with one-man shows in London, around Britain and Nigeria. He also joined group exhibitions in the US and UK.

Rotimi's work was called "fresh, challenging, sometimes irreverent". While specialising in the male nude, he also maintained a keen interest in his

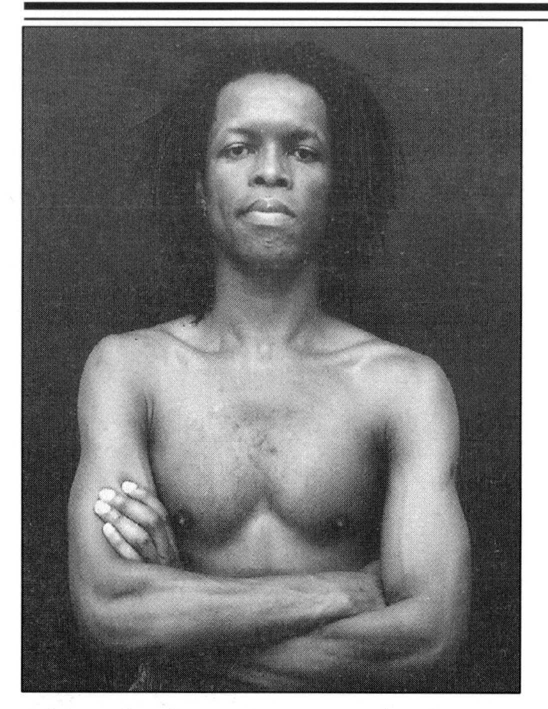

African heritage, incorporating images of Yoruba civilisation in his pictures. Recurring themes were desire, forbidden dreams and the contrast of differing cultures and traditions. He wrote of his work at length in 'Traces of Ecstasy' published in *Ten.8* (Journal of Photography) No. 28.

In 1983 he met the writer Alex Hirst, who became his life partner. They collaborated on two exhibitions, *Bodies of Experience* and *Ecstatic Antibodies*, addressing the issue of AIDS (Hirst was HIV positive). Hirst also provided the introduction for Rotimi's collection *Black Male / White Male*, published 1988.

Rotimi was described as quietly industrious, working with great concentration and technical skill. Generous in his help and encouragement to other photographers, he was active in the Brixton Artists' Collective and was a driving force in setting up, then chairing, the Association of Black Photographers (AUTOGRAPH).

Rotimi died of septicaemia 21 December 1989, aged only 34. One year later a retrospective of his work was shown at the 198 Gallery, Herne Hill; and 151 Railton Road was renamed Rotimi Fani-Kayode House, with a bronze plaque installed. A memorial lecture was held at the Photographers Gallery on 16 January 1991. Alex Hirst later brought out *The Last Supper: A creative farewell to Rotimi Fani-Kayode*, staged further exhibitions and published other books celebrating the art of his late lover.

## Charles Digby Fearon (1873-1902) Factory Inspector
## Robert Burton Fearon (1871-1902) Church Minister
## 103 Norwood Road

Charles and Robert Fearon were sons of a solicitor, Francis Fearon, who lived from c1885 to 1909 at Stanhope Lodge, a large detached early Victorian house at 103 Norwood Road. Robert was Vicar of the Church of St John the Evangelist, Hammersmith. Charles was Home Office Inspector of Factories, part of the small (c150) team of Inspectors with the difficult responsibility of ensuring employee health and safety in over a quarter of a million work-places.

Francis Fearon and his sons were keen mountaineers and members of the Alpine Club. On 20 August 1902, Charles and Robert climbed the Wetterhorn in Switzerland. The conditions were hazardous, and when they reached the summit, they and their guides were tragically killed by lightning. Rather ironically, Charles's work was concerned with electrical safety.

***Mounts Wetterhorn and Wellhorn from a sketch by John Ruskin***

Stanhope Lodge has now disappeared; the site is occupied by five terraced houses, built 1956-57.

There is a memorial tablet to the brothers in St Paul's Church, Herne Hill:

> In memory of Charles Digby Fearon H. M. Inspector of Factories, for 18 years a worshipper at this church who, with his brother Revd. Robert Burton Fearon and two guides, was killed by lightening on the summit of the Wetterhorn Mountain, Switzerland, 20th August 1902, Aged 29 years.
>
> 'A MAN GREATLY BELOVED' Dan. xii
>
> This tablet was erected by his Colleagues of the Factory Department, Home Office.

## James Fosbery (c1795-1884) 89 Dulwich Road Postman and Church Founder

In 1836, Leicester born postman James Fosbery and his wife Mary opened their home for 'cottage meetings' of the local branch of the United Methodist Free Church. It was at one of these meetings, in 1851, that William Booth (1829-1912), later to found the Salvation Army, met Catherine Mumford (1829-90), then living with her family in Russell Street, north Brixton. Booth, at that time a Methodist lay preacher, had come that day to preach. He worked full-time as a shop assistant in a pawnbroker's shop in Walworth. The couple married 16 June 1855 at the Stockwell New Chapel.

The Fosberys' house in Water Lane (renamed Dulwich Road in the 1850s) appears on all the census returns from 1841 to 1881. The address became 89 Dulwich Road in 1875 and was on the site now occupied by the grassed area in front of Park View House, between Regent Road and Hurst Street.

In 1869 the 'cottage meetings' stopped when the congregation found a site nearby at 25-27 Milton Road and erected a 'tin chapel' there. This chapel was superseded in 1875 by the first Methodist Church building in Railton Road. In 1883 James Fosbery, then aged 88, was presented with a large-print copy of the Psalms in appreciation of his dedicated service to the church. He died 4 July 1884 and is buried in Norwood Cemetery. After his death, the house at 89 Dulwich Road was demolished and a new church, Dulwich Road Methodist Church, was built on the site, opening in 1887.

***James Fosbery and his wife Mary***

## William Sutton Gover (1822-94) Casino House, 3 Herne Hill Actuary

W S Gover, son of William Gover of Lee Park, Kent and Mary Ann of Chelsea, was born 17 November 1822 in Old Kent Road. A Fellow of the Institute of Actuaries and of the Statistical Society, he was Secretary and Actuary of the British Empire Mutual Life Assurance Company. On 15 July 1854 he founded the British Equitable Assurance Company at 47 King William Street, London. His father was Chairman until his death in 1868. William was Managing Director from 1860-94, and the family connection continued until 1930. British Equitable, which had an accumulated fund of £1,141,810, merged with the State Assurance Company in 1922, two years later becoming part of the Royal Exchange Group, now the Guardian Royal Exchange.

Active in the City of London, from 1867 Gover joined the Court of Common Council for Vintry Ward. He became Deputy in 1891, when it was unanimously resolved heartily to congratulate him on his election for the 25th consecutive year, with "sincere thanks for his past services, not only to this ward, but to the public ... in the many positions of trust that he has been called upon to occupy".

*Casino House c1800*

William was a member of the London School Board from 1870-73 and 1876-82 and Chairman of the City Commission of Sewers 1874-75. In addition, he was a Director of House Property and Investment Company, founded 1876 "for the purchase and sale of productive and progressive house property, and improving the dwellings of the working classes on the self-supporting principle." He served as Chairman from 1886-94.

About 1880, he moved from the family residence, Havering House, Blackheath, to Casino House, designated 3 Herne Hill in 1883. There he lived with his wife, Maria, his mother, four daughters (including the artist Agnes L Gover), four sons including a barrister, an architect and an actuary, plus a niece and six (later seven) servants. W S Gover died at Casino House 24 November 1894 and was interred in the family vault at Nunhead Cemetery. Casino House stood empty until 1906, when it was demolished.

## Christopher Graham (1765-1847) 62 Herne Hill Grocer: An Unpleasant Death

Christopher Graham was for many years the chief partner in the firm of North, Simpson, Graham and Co., grocers and tea-dealers of 36 New Bridge Street, Blackfriars and of 190 Fleet Street. His large detached house, 62 Herne Hill (later called The Cedars, demolished in the 1890s) was located opposite St Paul's Church. However, it was set back from the main road to where Woodquest Avenue now runs between Gubyon and Kestrel Avenues.

***Premises of North, Simpson & Graham, New Bridge Street, late 1830s***

His death was reported in the *Gentleman's Magazine* of April 1847 as follows:

> "8 March. Aged 82, Christopher Graham, esq. of Herne Hill, Surrey...........His death was hastened by an embrocation having been unfortunately administered instead of a draught."

A detailed report appeared in *The Times* of Thursday 11 March 1847, after a coroner's inquest had convened on the Tuesday evening at the Prince Regent Inn (now the Prince Regent public house in Dulwich Road). There were two main witnesses called at the inquest. The first was footman Henry Keniance, who stated that "his master had been very ill latterly with lumbago." On the Monday morning a female servant came to him and said "Master is very bad, and stuff they have sent him to take almost choked him, as he was 29 minutes in taking it." The footman ran up to the bedroom and found that the wrong medicine had been given. Mrs Graham was told and she immediately ordered Mr English be sent for. The footman said that "the servant who administered the lotion was in the habit of being called to their bedchamber at all times of the night, and on the present unfortunate occasion she had in haste taken up the wrong bottle."

The second witness was the surgeon, Arthur William English of Forest Hill, who stated that "he found the deceased gentleman in a partial state of coma" and withdrew the contents of his stomach with a stomach-pump. A large quantity of embrocation or liniment had been taken, consisting of laudanum, camphor and ammonia. Mr Graham died about noon.

The coroner, William Carter, remarked on the deplorable nature of the affair, after which the jury agreed to a verdict of Accidental Death. Christopher Graham is interred in the catacombs of Norwood Cemetery.

## Euphemia Chalmers Gray (1828-97)
## 30 Herne Hill
## Wife of John Ruskin

Born in Perth on 7 May 1828, 'Effie' Gray was the pretty daughter of Scottish friends of the Ruskin family. George Gray, Effie's father, was a business associate of John James

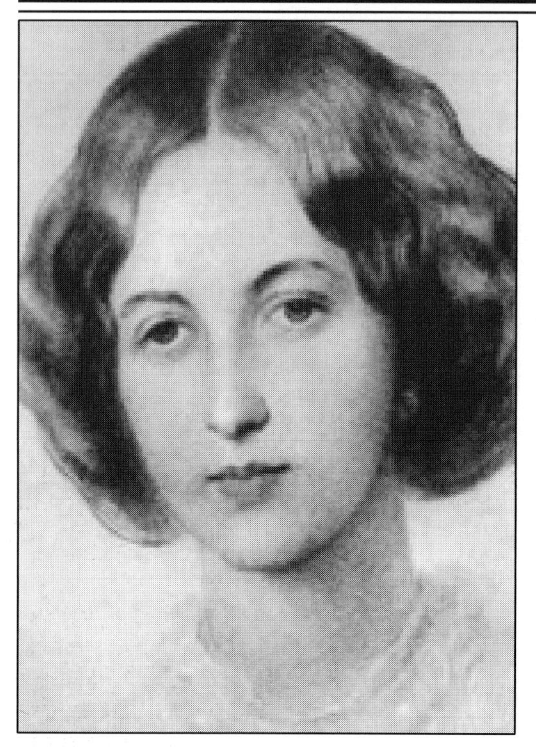

Ruskin. Effie first met John Ruskin when she was twelve, on a visit to Herne Hill in 1840. The following year, on a second visit, she challenged him to write a fairy story. *The King of the Golden River* (first published 1851) was Ruskin's only published fiction and became one of his most popular books. He began to show an interest in Effie when, aged 19, she came to stay at the Ruskins' Denmark Hill house. During a visit to Scotland he called on the Grays at their home in Perth and, returning to Herne Hill, wrote to Effie proposing marriage. She accepted and they married in Perth 10 April 1848 after hesitant encouragement from his parents.

This is an extract from a love letter from John to Effie:

> "You are like the bright - soft-swelling - lovely fields of a high glacier covered with fresh morning snow - which is heavenly to the eye - and soft and winning on the foot - but beneath, there are winding clefts and dark places in its cold - cold ice - where men fall, and rise not again."

The couple returned from their honeymoon to live at the Denmark Hill house. Even after they had moved to a rented property at 31 Park Street, Mayfair, Ruskin continued to work in his study at his parents' home.

Outwardly the couple appeared happy; but they lived a celibate marriage for six years. When John and Effie visited the Brownings, Elizabeth Barrett Browning described her as "naturally sprightly" and "pretty and exquisitely dressed."

Whilst travelling in Venice, where John researched for volumes two and three of his book *The Stones of Venice*, one of Effie's social triumphs was being received by Field-Marshal Count Radetzky and given his autographed picture.

She had much more interest in social than political affairs and would often describe her life in letters to her parents. Effie waited for John to 'marry' her, as he promised he would on her 25th birthday. Eventually, however, she went to her parents as friction developed between the two families. In February 1849 Effie returned to Perth and did not see her husband for nine months: he spent the summer in Switzerland with his mother and father.

In 1852 John and Effie moved to a house at 30 Herne Hill, next door to his previous home. John had for some time been involved with the Pre-Raphaelite circle, championing in particular John Everett Millais. Effie had posed for Millais as the wife of the freed Jacobite prisoner in his painting *The Order of*

*Release*, shown at the Royal Academy in 1853. In the summer of that year John invited Millais to holiday with them in Scotland, during which he was commissioned to produce the famous full-length portrait of Ruskin standing above a rocky stream. It was also during this holiday that a strong and sympathetic mutual attraction developed between Millais and Effie.

By autumn 1853 it was clear to Effie that John did not intend to consummate their marriage; conversely, he knew and apparently approved of his wife's affair with Millais. Relations with her in-laws had completely broken down; but it was not until the following year, on 25 April 1854, that Effie left Ruskin for good. Millais had by then been elected an associate member of the Royal Academy with an assured future (he later became its President).

In July Effie's father instigated proceedings against which John refused to defend himself. In 1854, the ecclesiastical commissary court of Surrey annulled the marriage on the grounds that "the said John Ruskin was incapable of consummating the same by reason of incurable impotency." However, the charge against him had to be attested to by a physical examination of Effie. The annulment was a scandal and Queen Victoria was so shocked by a wife leaving her husband that she refused to receive this woman at court, until Millais made a final request on his deathbed.

Effie married Millais in 1855 and bore him eight children. He used to refer to her as "The Countess". On 23 December 1897, she died as Lady Millais, having been the wife to two famous men.

## Donald Honey Grist (1891-1986)
## 35 Dorchester Court
## Agriculturalist

Donald Honey Grist was born in Huntingdon 11 February 1891. He studied at Cambridge University, gaining a Diploma in Agriculture. In his early twenties he went to the Far East, spending many years in Malaya, where he worked for the Colonial Agricultural Service. In 1942, Donald and his wife Isobel were living in Singapore when the Japanese captured the island. They were taken prisoner, separated and spent the rest of the war suffering considerable hardship as civilian internees.

Donald's professional interest was in tropical agriculture. He was well known as a consultant and writer, publishing a large number of scientific articles and books on many aspects of the subject. However, he was particularly celebrated for his knowledge and expertise in the area of rice cultivation, where he was one of the world's greatest experts. His two books, *Rice* (1955) and, co-authored with R J A W Lever, *Pests of Rice* (1969) are regarded as seminal works on the subject.

***Rice plant (Oryza Sativa)***

Donald was made a Fellow of the Linnaean Society in 1961 and was awarded an OBE in 1977 for his work in the field of tropical agriculture. He and Isobel moved to 35 Dorchester Court in 1964 and lived there until his death on 7 July 1986.

## Joseph Gurney (1804-79)
## 180 Denmark Hill
## Shorthand Writer

Joseph Gurney was the fourth generation of Gurney shorthand writers and the eldest son of William Brodie Gurney. His father and grandfather Joseph had both been well known and successful in the field; young Joseph must have inherited their talents and skills.

Joseph was born in London 15 October 1804. Little is known about his childhood; however, by 1822 aged 18, he was acting as secretary to a House of Commons committee. In 1849, when his father resigned as shorthand writer to the Houses of Parliament, Joseph replaced him.

Like his father, Joseph Gurney was active in religious and charitable works. He was a member of the Religious Tract Society and Treasurer of the Regent's Park Baptist College. He also published a number of popular biblical commentaries and, in 1877, the *Revised English Bible*.

In 1872 he retired from his post in the Houses of Parliament, the job passing to his nephew, William Henry Gurney Salter.

Joseph was married twice: first to Emma (d 1842), with whom he had several children; and then to Harriet, who bore him two sons, William and Joseph John. In the late 1830s he was living at 180 Denmark Hill (now numbered 164). The present house is much altered since Joseph lived there.

On 12 August 1879, Joseph died at his then home, Tyndale Lodge, Wimbledon Common. He is buried in Norwood Cemetery.

## William Brodie Gurney (1777-1855)
## 170 Denmark Hill
## Shorthand Writer
## and Philanthropist

William Brodie Gurney was born in Stamford Hill 24 December 1777. William's grandfather, Thomas Gurney (1705-70), had invented a system of shorthand, or brachyography, publishing many books on the subject. Thomas had been shorthand writer to the Government, and his system was commonly used for reporting of both Houses of Parliament. Using the same system Thomas's son Joseph (1744-1815), also a shorthand writer, reported the celebrated 1788 trial of Warren Hastings. Later Charles Dickens also reported sessions of Parliament using the Gurney system.

William, following his grandfather's and father's footsteps, began practice as a shorthand writer in 1803. He reported on many trials, appeals, courts-martial and libel cases, including the impeachment of Lord

*Gurney shorthand system: part of Psalm 113*

Melville (1805), the proceedings against the Duke of York (1809), the trials of Lord Cochrane (1814) and Lord Thislewood (1820) and, in the same year, the proceedings against Queen Caroline. In 1802, together with his father, William was appointed to take notes of evidence before the committees of the Houses of Lords and Commons. In 1813 he was formally appointed shorthand writer to both Houses of Parliament. William was paid two guineas a day for attendance, and one shilling a folio for the transcript of his notes. William's fame was such that Byron, in his *Don Juan*, when referring to reports in the English papers of a Spanish divorce case, wrote the line: "the best is that in short-hand ta'en by Gurney".

In addition to his professional shorthand writing, William was well known for his philanthropic works. He was a founder-member, Secretary, Treasurer (for over 30 years) and later President of the Sunday School Union and editor of its successful journal *The Youth's Magazine*. William devoted the large profits from this to educational and missionary institutions. He took Sunday church services, was on the board of the London Female Penitentiary and on the committee of the Westminster Branch of the British and Foreign Bible Society. He was also Treasurer of Stepney College from 1828. He was very involved with the anti-slavery movement, contributing towards building several chapels in Jamaica. William's publications included *A Lecture to Children and Youth on the History and Characters of Heathen Idolatry, with Some References to the Effects of Christian Missions* (1848). He also edited the 15th and 16th editions of his grandfather's book *Brachyography*.

The Gurney shorthand method was later superseded by less cumbersome systems, such as Pitman (1837) and Gregg (1888).

William moved to 170 Denmark Hill c1831 and lived there until his death on 25 March 1855. Thirty-two family members are listed on his tombstone in Norwood Cemetery. The house was demolished c1906 when Ruskin Park was established.

## Joseph Gutteridge (1752-1844)
## Denmark Hill
## Philanthropist

The death of Joseph Gutteridge was reported in the *Gentleman's Magazine* of June 1844 as follows:

> "May 12. At Denmark-hill, aged 91, John (*sic*) Gutteridge, esq. He was one of the founders of the Sunday School Society, and for more than half a century a zealous promoter of various

religious and benevolent institutions; among which may be named the Baptist Fund, Stepney College, the Baptist Mission, the Widows' Fund, and the Dissenting Deputies."

In 1813, at the time of the review of the East India Charter, Joseph secured the clause protecting the missionaries of the Baptist Missionary Society. In 1822 he helped Denmark Place Baptist Church, Coldharbour Lane, to buy the lease of their building, putting the church on a sound financial footing. In 1823 he recommended Edward Steane (1798-1882) as their minister. Steane held the post until 1861; and under his pastoral care the church flourished.

Joseph was born in Leighton Buzzard, Bedfordshire and lived at Denmark Hill from the 1790s until his death on 12 May 1844. His house was located on the site of the present Parkside Nursery between Ruskin Park and King's College Hospital. The house was demolished in the 1860s to make way for the railway which opened in 1866.

## Captain James Horsburgh (1762-1836)
## 37 Herne Hill
## Hydrographer and Chart Maker

Born in Scotland, James Horsburgh was apprenticed aged 16 to a firm which operated ships in the North Sea coal trade. After then gaining experience in the China Sea during a succession of voyages for Bombay ship owners, he decided to live in India, where in 1798 he was appointed to his own command.

During his adventurous, sea-faring career, Horsburgh developed an interest in scientific observations and charting. Whilst sailing between India and China, he collected information

***Horsburgh Memorial in St Paul's Church, Herne Hill***

and observations about the navigation of the eastern seas. After meeting in London with Alexander Dalrymple, Hydrographer to the East India Company, three of his first charts were published: *The Straits of Macasser, The Western Philippines* and *The Tract from Dampier's Strait to Batavia*. Horsburgh then provided Dalrymple with a 'book of remarks', later published as *Observations on the Eastern Seas* (1799).

Many of Horsburgh's privately published charts were taken over by the Hydrographic Office and issued as Admiralty Charts. These included *The Malacca Strait, The China Sea* and *Bombay Harbour*, together with the explanatory text, *Memoirs Comprising the Navigation to and from China*.

Horsburgh retired in 1804 and returned to Britain. He was elected a Fellow of the Royal Society in March 1806.

In 1805, aged 43, Horsburgh married Elizabeth Longworth and settled at 6 Saville Row, Walworth. The house became 143 Walworth Road in 1865, now the site of the petrol station beside Wansey Street. Only eight years after the birth of their third child, Elizabeth died suddenly in 1829. She was buried in Dulwich Old Burial Ground.

From the 1820s until his own death in 1836, from hydrothorax, Horsburgh lived at 37 Herne Hill, the present site of Denesmede flats. It is possible that this house, which became No 131 Herne Hill in 1913, was destroyed during WW2 when St Paul's church was also bombed.

Horsburgh's will states that he owned a property in Brighton and that he requested to be buried next to his wife in Dulwich. Although built after his death, St Paul's Church, Herne Hill contains a memorial to Captain James Horsburgh. The first lighthouse in Singapore, standing on the Rock of Pedro Branca, was named after him.

## Joe Hunte (c1918-83)
## 43 Cambria Road
## Social Reformer and Activist

Joe Hunte was born in St Vincent around 1918, moving with his parents to Trinidad some three years later. He worked as a teacher before coming to England in 1958 to study Politics, Economics and Philosophy at Swansea University. He was active in college politics and won the Observer Mace in the newspaper's annual student debating competition.

After graduating, Joe became a Public Relations Officer at the University. He was later called to the Bar, though he never practised as a barrister. While working in Swansea he met his future wife Ann, a student at the University. They married in September 1967 and had two children - Joanne (who sadly died of an asthma attack when only twelve years old) and Sarah.

Ann and Joe came to live in Brixton; and for a short time Joe worked in the Civil Service. In 1968, he took the post of Senior Community Relations Officer in Tower Hamlets, a position he held until he retired in 1982. His work with the Bangladeshi community was largely instrumental in helping avoid the inter-racial tensions that occurred in other parts of London. In 1970 Ann and Joe moved to 43 Cambria Road, and were still living there when Joe died.

Joe was always very active in issues affecting the West Indian community. He wrote extensively on education and housing, and the expectations and experiences of West Indian immigrants. He was appointed to the Home Office advisory committee dealing with race and immigration, was a committee member of the Joint

Council for the Welfare of Immigrants and of the Anne Frank Foundation. From 1958 until his death he was Chair and Secretary of the West Indian Standing Conference.

In the 1960s Joe was attending an event in Lambeth Town Hall, where an incident occurred that provoked a serious over-reaction on the part of the police. As a result of this experience, Joe wrote a pamphlet *Nigger Hunting in England?* published in 1967 by the West Indian Standing Conference. In his pamphlet, Joe discusses the reasons for mutual suspicion between immigrants and the police and for the feelings amongst immigrants that police actions towards them stem mainly from the colour of their skins. He suggested that it was police misunderstanding and misinterpretations about immigrant communities that gave rise to prejudice. Joe's solutions included more coloured policemen at all levels in the service; interchange with black commonwealth countries to learn more about immigrants' background and cultures; more police involvement with local groups, and better police training and involvement of immigrant organisations in that training.

Joe's pamphlet had a very significant impact on reforming police training and attitudes; and the ideas he put forward are now standard practice. Joe was afterwards frequently invited to lecture to trainees and serving police officers on community relations issues.

Joe was very sociable and also liked a drink. It was after a visit to the nearby Cambria Arms that he collapsed and died suddenly outside his home on 8 October 1983. He was buried at Norwood Cemetery; his gravestone shows two hands, one black and one white, symbolically clasped together. Another memorial to him is Joe Hunte Court, a sheltered housing scheme just off Knight's Hill, in a close named after St Vincent, the island of his birth.

Joe's philosophy is best summed up in his own words: "In a democracy the Government of the day has a responsibility to create an environment in which all its people - irrespective of race, colour, class, creed, sexuality, or disability - are given equal access to education and to participate equally in the creation of the wealth of the nation."

## Sir Robert Hunter (1844-1913)
## 10 de Crespigny Terrace
## Lawyer and National Trust Founder

Robert Hunter was born at 3 Addington Square, Camberwell, 27 October 1844. He was the elder of two children of Robert Lachlan Hunter, master mariner and ship-owner and his wife, Anne. After gaining a first class honours degree, and in 1865 an MA from University College, he qualified as a lawyer.

In 1869, he became a partner in the firm of Fawcett, Home and Hunter, solicitors to the Commons Preservation Society, which had been set up to prevent illegal enclosure of open spaces. Robert's most notable case, lasting from 1871 to 1874, was to act on behalf of the City of London Corporation to recover 3,000 acres of Epping Forest from enclosure. Public opinion had been roused against the enclosure of many London commons. Robert led other actions resulting in the protection of Hampstead Heath, Berkhamsted, Plumstead, and Wimbledon commons and other threatened open spaces. He also helped establish the principles of public interest on which the law relating to commons is now based.

Sir Robert's first wife, Emily Browning, died in childbirth. On 19 May 1877 he married Ellen Cann (1851-1932) with whom he had three daughters. In 1882 he was appointed solicitor to the General Post Office, holding that position until shortly before his death. In this role he dealt with over fifty Acts of Parliament. Most notably, he negotiated the Post Office's 1909 purchase of the national telephone system.

Despite Robert's successes in reversing many illegal enclosures, he realised that more effective methods were needed to deal with the actions of private landowners. So in 1884 he began to argue for the creation of a national organisation to acquire land and buildings and to hold them for the benefit of the nation. He went on to outline the guiding principles of what was to become in 1894 the 'National Trust for Places of Historic Interest or Natural Beauty'. Sir Robert, knighted that same year for his services to the conservation of open spaces, chaired the executive committee that drafted the 1907 National Trust Act. He continued to be actively involved with conservation issues until his death from septicaemia on 6 November 1913.

The 1861 census shows Robert Hunter living with his father, mother and sister at 10 de Crespigny Terrace. This was one of a terrace of twelve houses in Champion Park, between Denmark Hill and Windsor Walk, in what is now part of the grounds of the Salvation Army's William Booth College. The house was bombed in WW2 and subsequently demolished. After living in Kingston and in Putney, in 1881 Hunter bought Meadfields Hanger. This was a substantial property in Haslemere, Surrey, where he stayed for the rest of his life.

## William Innes (1905-99)
## 38 Ruskin Walk
## Artist

William Innes was born 23 February 1905. He began work in 1926 as a shorthand typist with tile makers Carter and Co. near the Albert Embankment. Apart from war service as an RAF radar operator, he stayed with this company until his retirement in 1971. By then he was a director, responsible for the tiling needs of many client companies including Lyons, Kodak and Sainsbury's.

William was a self-taught artist, and after retirement began a successful second career as a painter in oils and watercolours. He was elected President of the London Sketch Club, honorary life member of the Pastel Society Council and member of the United Society of Artists. His work has been hung at the Royal Academy, the Royal Society of British Artists, the Royal Institute of Oil Painters and the Royal

Society of Marine Artists. He also spent much of his time helping young artists.

In 1968 William moved to 38 Ruskin Walk with his wife Violet (b 1908). After Violet's death in 1979, William continued to live in the house until he died on 5 November 1999.

## Thomas Owen Jacobsen (1864-1941)
## 3 Stradella Road & 99 Herne Hill
## Stationer and MP

Born in Liverpool, Thomas Owen Jacobsen was the fourth of eleven children of a Danish merchant father and an Irish mother. At the time of the 1881 census, he was described as a stationers' apprentice, aged 16. In 1893 he set up in his own business and from c1896-1936 was Chairman of the wholesale stationery company Jacobsen & Welch of 7 Paternoster Square, London, with additional premises at Liverpool and Glasgow. He travelled extensively for the company, and claimed to have been seven times around the world. From 1925-27 he was President of the Federation of Envelope Makers and Manufacturing Stationers; and from 1929-31, President of the Stationers' Association of Great Britain.

In 1916 Thomas was elected unopposed as Liberal MP for the Hyde division of Cheshire, but lost his seat in 1918. He unsuccessfully contested South-East Southwark in 1921, Lambeth Kennington in 1923, and the City of London in 1929. From 1919-21 he sat as Councillor for North Lambeth on the LCC.

In 1890 he married Annie Amelie Pauline Veillard, the daughter of a banker. From 1910-20 they lived at 3 Stradella Road and from 1921-27 at 99 Herne Hill, former home of Richard Muir. Thomas died at Worthing on 15 June 1941, just three weeks after the death of his wife. They had no children.

## C L R James (1901-89)
## 165 Railton Road
## Writer and Political Philosopher

Cyril Lionel Robert James was born at Tunapuna near Port of Spain, Trinidad 4 January 1901. His father was a schoolteacher, his mother an avid reader. Their house was situated behind the wicket; by standing on a chair at his bedroom window, the boy could watch cricket practice every evening and matches on Saturdays. This profoundly influenced his outlook on life and his future career.

James studied history, culture and literature at Queen's Royal College, but rebelled against the formality and authority there. In the 1920s he became a cricket reporter; he also began to write fiction showing the vitality of back street life: *La Divina Pastora* (1927) and *Triumph* (1929). He sailed to England in 1932, joining cricketer Learie Constantine in Nelson, Lancashire. Acting as Constantine's amanuensis, James also published *The Case for West Indian Self-Government* and established himself as a cricket writer for the *Manchester Guardian*.

Moving to London in 1933, James became a leading figure in the Trotskyist movement. He produced many works, including the novel *Minty Alley*, *Abyssinia and the Imperialists*, the play *Toussaint L'Ouverture* (staged 1936, starring Paul Robeson) and *The Black Jacobins*.

In 1938 he went on a speaking tour to the United States, and remained for 15 years. He met Constance Webb in 1939, and began a loving correspondence;

they married in 1948. In America he wrote important works, particularly on the race question. Deported in 1953, he returned to Trinidad, where he edited *The Nation* and published his autobiography, *Beyond a Boundary* (1963). He initially helped the newly independent country's first President, Eric Williams. However, arrested and expelled for opposing Williams in the 1966 elections, James travelled widely in Africa before returning to the United States. For more than a decade he taught and spoke on contemporary issues while writing on cultural figures. Though his marriage was dissolved, he continued corresponding with Webb all his life.

In 1981 James returned to London, where he lived simply and quietly above the offices of *Race Today*, at 165 Railton Road. Generous with practical advice to visitors, he was famed as a widely influential elder statesman. His Channel 4 lectures in 1983 covered a range of topics and displayed acute analysis, vitality and a profoundly humane vision. James died 31 May 1989. An English Heritage Blue Plaque was unveiled in 2004 on the Shakespeare Road side of his final home.

## Harry Jones (1866-1925)
## 29 Half Moon Lane
## Journalist

Harry Jones was born in Llanelly, South Wales, on 27 March 1866. He began work as a journalist, eventually becoming Assistant Editor of the *South Wales Daily News*, and later Editor of the *Weekly Sun*. In 1897 he went to Plymouth as managing editor of the *Western Daily Mercury*. Seven years later he came to London to become Deputy Editor of the *Daily Chronicle*. He also found time to study law and was called to the bar in May 1906.

In 1918, following a dispute with the *Daily Chronicle*'s owners over his criticisms of Lloyd George, Harry moved to become Parliamentary correspondent at the *Daily News*.

In 1895, Harry married Emily Margaret Mainwaring. They had one son, Paul, born in 1896. Paul was killed on 31 July 1917, while serving in the Royal Tank Corps, shot in the head by a sniper firing through a porthole in his tank.

By 1918, Harry and Emily were living at 29 Half Moon Lane. They remained there until Harry's death on 11 January 1925.

## Kennedy Jones (1865-1921)
## 15 Stradella Road
## Joint Founder, the *Daily Mail*

Born 4 May 1865 in Glasgow, William Kennedy Jones began in journalism at the age of 16. He worked on the *Glasgow News* and later on the *Glasgow Evening News* where he became Assistant Editor. In the early

1890s he was working as Assistant Editor on the *Birmingham Daily Mail.*

On moving to London, KJ, as he was known, managed to acquire an option on the *Evening News*, which was then running at a loss despite a good circulation of 100,000. In 1895, with himself as Editor he persuaded Alfred Harmsworth (later Lord Northcliffe, 1865-1922), then with little newspaper experience, to buy the paper. KJ refashioned the newspaper by reducing political news, increasing sports coverage and introducing feature articles and prize competitions. With the introduction of short, snappy paragraphs, the circulation quadrupled in just a few months.

In 1896 at KJ's suggestion, Harmsworth started a new newspaper, to be the first tabloid in Britain, called the *Daily Mail.* KJ was given overall responsibility for content and style of the new paper while remaining as Editor of the *Evening News.* With its readership coming mostly from the lower middle classes, the *Daily Mail*'s circulation reached one million by the time of the Boer War (1899-1902). The paper became known as "A Penny Paper for One Halfpenny". Although it cost more than a halfpenny to produce, it was the first British newspaper to be dependent mainly on advertising.

In 1900 KJ relinquished the editorship of the *Evening News*, but remained the deputy and right-hand man to Harmsworth. In 1908 it was KJ who led the negotiations on Harmsworth's purchase of *The Times*. He modernised the newspaper's printing works but was disappointedly kept out of editorial decisions. In 1912 KJ retired from journalism and sold his newspaper interests. He undertook the financial reorganisation of the London furniture store Waring and Gillow, serving as Chairman until 1914.

Although politically a Unionist, KJ stood in two Parliamentary by-elections in 1916 as an independent: first at Wimbledon and second, successfully, at Hornsey. In 1917 he took an unpaid appointment as Director-General of the Food Economy Department of the Ministry of Food. In 1919 he served as Chairman of the Select Committee on Transport (Metropolitan Area).

In 1892 he married Hetty Staniland in Birmingham; they had one son and three daughters. In 1896 the family moved to 15 Stradella Road, then newly built. They stayed for about three years and then removed to Finchley. After an illness of a few months, KJ died of pneumonia, aged 56, on 20 October 1921 and was cremated at Golders Green Crematorium. He left £206,537 in his will.

## Prof. Reginald Victor Jones (1911-97)
## 133 Shakespeare Road, 188 and 194 Railton Road
## Physicist

One of Britain's foremost scientists, Reginald Jones CH CB CBE FRS made some of the most important contributions to physics, to science teaching and to the secret intelligence war during WW2.

The son of Harold Victor Jones, a sergeant in the Grenadier Guards, and his wife Alice, Reginald Jones was born 29 September 1911 at 188 Railton Road. By 1920 the family had moved to 133 Shakespeare Road; but in 1931 they went to live at 194 Railton Road. Reginald attended St Jude's School until he was eight years of age, when he transferred to the Sussex Road

School. In 1922 he won a scholarship to Alleyn's School and later an open exhibition to study physics at Wadham College, Oxford. There he gained a First and a grant to work for a doctorate.

After work at the Clarendon Laboratory on radar and infrared aircraft detection, in 1939 Reginald took an appointment as Scientific Officer at the Air Ministry, eventually becoming Assistant Director of the RAF Intelligence Section. Reginald's explanation of how German bombers located their targets using intersecting radio beams, his work on interpreting Enigma code messages, on radar, and analysing the flood of intelligence about the V1 and the V2, were all of immense importance to the defence of Britain. Among his many successful ideas was 'window' - strips of metallic foil dropped from bombers to confuse enemy ground radar. Winston Churchill said that he was "someone who did more to save us from disaster than many who are glittering with trinkets." In 1940 Reginald married Vera Cain; they had two daughters and a son.

In 1946 Reginald was appointed Professor of Natural Philosophy at the University of Aberdeen, a post he held until his retirement in 1981. During his time at Aberdeen, much of his work focused on improving the sensitivity of scientific instruments. He was awarded a CBE in 1942, CB in 1946, elected a Fellow of the Royal Society in 1965 and made a Companion of Honour in 1994. The Yorkshire Television documentary series *The Secret War of Dr Jones* was based on his book *Most Secret War*.

In 1993 the CIA honoured him with a perpetual intelligence medal in his name. George J Tenet, the CIA's Director of Central Intelligence, spoke of R V Jones as "an extraordinarily gifted scientist whose ingenuity and resourcefulness contributed greatly to the Allied victory in WW2."

Reginald never lost his affection for Herne Hill and stayed in touch with many of the people he had known there as a child. He died suddenly of a cardiac arrest at a hospital in Aberdeen 17 December 1997 aged 86.

Electoral records show Reginald living with his parents at 194 Railton Road until the war years. Harold died c1953, but Alice remained at the house until it was demolished in the mid-1960s, to make way for the present block of flats built by Lambeth Council.

## Dorothy Kerin (1889-1963)
## 204 Milkwood Road
## 'Miracle Lady'

In 1902, following the death of her father, Dorothy Kerin moved with her mother Emily from Walworth to 204 Milkwood Road.

Dorothy's is the story of 'The Miracle of Herne Hill'. As a child, she suffered for many years from tubercular

meningitis, then a serious and intractable illness. On 18 February 1912, having lost consciousness and pronounced on the verge of death, she made an immediate and unexplained recovery. Sixteen people are said to have witnessed her stand up and walk across the room, perfectly healed. This recovery, it is said, was accompanied by visions and the voices of angels singing that were heard throughout the house.

As a result of extensive local and national press coverage, Dorothy became famous. She continued to hear voices and see visions; and she later noted that stigmata appeared. Media interest was so great that she had to leave Milkwood Road to avoid the crowds round her home.

Dorothy gained a reputation as a healer and in 1929 she opened a 'Home of Healing', St Raphael's in Ealing. This was the first of a number of such establishments in that part of London. Later she raised the money needed to found, in 1948, 'Burrswood', a Christian healing centre near Tunbridge Wells, that is still functioning today.

Dorothy died on 26 January 1963 and was buried in St John's Churchyard, Groombridge, Kent. The house at 204 Milkwood Road was demolished in the 1960s. The site is immediately opposite 169 Milkwood Road and near the Milkwood Community Park.

## Sir John Key, Bart (1794-1858)
## 172 Denmark Hill
## Lord Mayor of London

Born 16 August 1794 in London, he was the eldest son of John Key (d 1821) of Key Brothers, wholesale stationers of 30 Abchurch Street and later 97 and 103 Newgate Street in the City of London. In 1818 John Jr entered the family business, and by 1830 had become Master of the Stationers Company. In 1823 he became Alderman of the Corporation of London for Langbourne Ward, and the following year was appointed Sheriff of London and Middlesex. In 1830 he served as Lord Mayor of London and, being one of the leading supporters of the Reform Bill, was unusually re-elected for a second term in 1831. In 1853 he resigned as an Alderman when elected Chamberlain of London, a post that paid the handsome salary of £2,500 a year.

John Key's mayoralty was marked by controversy. In 1830 while still mayor-elect, he wrote to the Prime Minister, the Duke of Wellington, warning him to provide a guard to his person when attending the Lord Mayor's Day celebrations. Key thought the Duke might be at risk of attack due to his unpopularity over his anti-Reform Bill policy. The letter resulted in King William IV being advised not to attend the celebrations; and great alarm spread around London. The Tower of London moat was flooded, the guards at the Bank of England doubled and the Lord Mayor's Show and Dinner cancelled. Key expressed his regret in having written the letter; however, the press had a field-day, describing him as "Don-Key." A number of cartoons were drawn showing caricatures of Key, dressed in mayoral robes, but with asses' ears, legs and hooves.

The following year, John Key, in his duties as Lord Mayor, escorted the King on his visit to the City for the official opening of the new London Bridge. The Duke of Wellington was among the large audience. The press was expecting another debacle, but the visit went well and Key was created a baronet.

In 1832 he was elected as Liberal MP for the City of London. However, his parliamentary career was brief and he resigned in 1833. It was alleged that his son had been appointed "without sufficient competition" to the post of Storekeeper and Superintendent of Stationery in His Majesty's Stationery Office.

In 1814 John Key married Charlotte, daughter of Francis and Sarah Green of Dorking and of 152 Denmark Hill – the site is now part of King's College Hospital. From 1814-32, the couple lived in a large mansion on Denmark Hill, possibly No.172 on a site now part of Ruskin Park near Ferndene Road. It had formerly been his father's house. They had two sons and three daughters. About 1833 they moved from Denmark Hill, and from 1852 were living at the Manor House, Streatham. John Key died, suffering from gout, at Streatham on 15 July 1858 and is buried in Norwood Cemetery.

## Sir Kingsmill Grove Key, Bart (1815-99) 172 Denmark Hill

The eldest son of Sir John Key, Kingsmill Grove Key was born 7 May 1815 in London, possibly at Denmark Hill, and educated at Mill Hill School. At one time he attended the school of the Rev. Thomas Dale (1797-1870) in Grove Lane, Camberwell where John Ruskin also went. Dale was Minister (1830-35) at St Matthew's Chapel, Denmark Hill.

*Kingsmill James Key*

In the 1830s Kingsmill moved with his parents from Denmark Hill to Hampstead. On the death of his father in 1858 he succeeded to the baronetcy. His entry in *Who's Who* described him as having "a very quiet career, chiefly devoted to scientific gardening and agricultural pursuits." From 1860-62 he was a captain in the 21st Essex Rifle Volunteers, also one of the first churchwardens at Immanuel Church, Streatham (built 1854). He showed a keen interest in cricket, which was obviously shared by his second son, Kingsmill James Key (1864-1932) who captained the Surrey County eleven from 1894-99.

Kingsmill Grove Key married four times and three of his wives predeceased him. He died on 28 December 1899 at The Rookery, Streatham, the home of his fourth wife, Jane, and is buried in Norwood Cemetery. His eldest son, the Rev. John Kingsmill Key (1853-1926), a missionary in Central Africa, succeeded to the baronetcy.

## Joyce Mildred Lambert (1916-2005)
## 50 Oakbank Grove
## Botanist

Joyce Mildred Lambert was born on 23 June 1916 at 50 Oakbank Grove, the only child of an estate agent father. Shortly afterwards the family moved to Norfolk where she attended Norwich High School for Girls. In 1939 she graduated in Botany from the University College of Wales, Aberystwyth.

After a time as a school teacher in Norwich, Joyce took up a lecturing post at Westfield College, London University. The focus of her research was the area of fenland bordering the river Yare in Norfolk. She showed that the Norfolk Broads, with almost perpendicular walls and flat floors were former peat diggings and man-made. She thus overturned the then commonly held view that the Broads were formed by natural processes. Her conclusions caused a sensation. A multi-disciplinary team, including Joyce, published their findings in a National Geographical Society memoir *The Making of the Broads* (1960).

In 1948 Joyce moved to Cambridge University and began to study the ecology of the Norfolk river Bure. In 1950 she was appointed lecturer in Botany at Southampton University, turning her attention to the salt marshes bordering Southampton water; and later to plant communities in the New Forest.

Joyce retired in 1979 and returned to live in the Yare valley house built by her grandfather in the early 1920s. Her last few years were spent in a

nursing home; but she still retained her close interest in the Broads.

Joyce Lambert never married. She died on 4 May 2005.

## William Leaf (1791-1874)
## 36 Herne Hill
## Art Collector

William Leaf was the son of William Leaf (1758-1830), formerly of Bishops Monkton, Yorkshire, and Susanna Ladler of Cripplegate, London. Leaf senior was a wholesale haberdasher and linen draper of Fleet Street, London. About 1810, Leaf junior joined his father's firm, by then at 39 Old Change, Cheapside, becoming a partner in 1820 when the firm was styled as Leaf, Son and Coles.

In 1815 William Leaf Jr married his cousin, Jane Leaf. Over the next 22 years they had eleven children. During the 1820s they lived at 36 Herne Hill, a semi-detached house whose site is now occupied by The Quadrangle.

The drapery business prospered, and in 1829 he bought Hill House, an early 18th century mansion at Streatham Common. He had the house demolished the following year and commissioned architect John B Papworth (1775-1847) to build a large Georgian style mansion, to be called Park Hill, affording grand views of the surrounding countryside. Papworth had designed many large houses in that style, including Brockwell Hall. William Leaf left his Herne Hill house for Park Hill in 1830, the same year as the death of his father, who had lived at Goose Green, East Dulwich.

William lived at Park Hill for the rest of his life, devoting his time to his business and the large family. He developed his interest in art and became a well-known collector; Park Hill was always full of drawings and paintings. In May 1875, after William's death, the auction sale of his collection at Christie's comprised 538 lots, took three days to complete and raised £32,357. The collection was remarkable for its size rather than quality. But there were some first-rate pieces that fetched high prices, including works by Turner, Prout, Barret, Robson, Haghe, Lewis, Gilbert, Nesfield, Roberts, Cattermole and Harding.

William Leaf died 3 July 1874 and is buried at Norwood Cemetery in a large family vault. Six years after his death, Park Hill became the home of Sir Henry Tate (1819-99), the sugar manufacturer and founder of the Tate Gallery.

## Luke Lightfoot (1721-89)
## Denmark Hall, Denmark Hill
## Woodcarver, Stonemason, Builder and Embezzler

Luke Lightfoot was christened 28 April 1721 at St Dunstan's Church, Stepney. In 1743 he received the freedom of the Draper's Company (by virtue of his father also having been a Freeman). At that time he was described as a carver, of Mile End Old Town.

In 1757 Luke advertised some marble chimney-pieces for sale. Ralph, 2nd Earl Verney (c1712-91), needed such stonework for his London house in Curzon Street and his country seat at Claydon, Buckinghamshire (National Trust since 1956). He visited Luke at his business premises, then at Gravel Lane in Southwark. The outcome of this meeting was that Lightfoot would supply Verney with all carved marble and stonework to a finished state and supply all other building materials "at very reasonable rates." Luke also offered to manage all Verney's building projects. Verney gullibly employed Luke, claiming him to be "very honest, able and skilful."

Luke's work on the south wing of Claydon House took him some ten years. Verney then appointed Sir Thomas Robinson (c1702-77) as architect for the rotunda and north wing. Robinson took a dislike to Luke, calling him "an ignorant knave, with no small spice of madness in his composition." However, Robinson continued to work with him for a year before realising that Luke was a fraudulent as well as an inefficient builder. Luke left Verney's service in 1769.

In 1771 Verney took Luke to court, accusing him of "gross neglect." He also claimed Luke had received £30,000 for works carried out which were valued at only £7,000. A compromise was reached whereby, in lieu of refunding the money, Luke assigned Verney the leases of some properties bought in the 1760s. It later emerged, however, that these properties were so badly constructed that they needed rebuilding. In 1784, after a number of unfortunate investments, Verney was declared bankrupt.

Despite his colourful personality, Luke Lightfoot did produce many extraordinary rococo carvings, in stone and in wood, for the interior decorations at Claydon House. They have since been described as "unmatched anywhere in England," yet no other examples of his work have ever been found.

In 1769 Luke built Denmark Hall (the site is now the Fox-on-the-Hill pub) as a place of entertainment, naming it in honour of the King of Denmark's visit to England the previous year. In his will, proved 25 November 1789, he described himself as a victualler of Lambeth (the Denmark Hall site was in Lambeth until boundary changes in 1900). His son, Theophilus Lightfoot (d 1841), continued the business after his father's death, but converted the premises into a number of leased dwellings. He used a smaller building as Tea Rooms, which proved more profitable. The road there was briefly known as Denmark Hall Hill, changing to Denmark Hill c1790.

## Zoë Linsley-Thomas (1935-2002)
## 198 Railton Road
## Gallery Director

Born 8 March 1935, Zoë was Director and co-founder, with her partner Noel Morgan, of the 198 Gallery in Railton

Road. They set up the Gallery after the December 1988 Brixton riots, with the aims of giving black artists a space to exhibit their work, and to reflect the multicultural communities that make up Lambeth and the surrounding boroughs.

A former mini-cab driver, Zoë had no strong associations with the art world. However, driven by her enthusiasm and strongly motivated by the needs of the local community - in particular those of young people - she worked tirelessly to make a positive contribution to their lives. She helped shape the careers of many artists, some of whom have become widely recognised for their achievements.

The 198 Gallery provides a platform for work reflecting the cultural diversity of British society and gives the opportunity to analyse and appreciate this work through interpretation and education. It has gained a wide reputation for innovative issues-based exhibitions and for its critically acclaimed work in the field of multicultural art education.

Zoë Linsley-Thomas died 11 August 2002 during a holiday to her daughter's home in France.

## Sir George Livesey (1834-1908)
## 50 Herne Hill
## Gas Engineer

George Thomas Livesey, born 8 April 1834, was the son of Thomas Livesey (1807-71) who from 1839 was manager of the South Metropolitan Gas Company, Old Kent Road, rising to Secretary (or Chief Executive) 1842-71. In that capacity, the father introduced a number of benefits for his workers including sickness and superannuation funds, and a week's holiday with pay.

In 1848, George Livesey was apprenticed to his father, later becoming the Assistant Manager (1857) and Engineer (1862). He succeeded his father as Secretary in 1871. Under George's management, new techniques for gas purification were introduced and the first of the very large gasholders built, greatly cutting storage costs. The company bought smaller, neighbouring gas companies (at Rotherhithe, Vauxhall and the Oval) and built new works at East Greenwich (the site of The Dome) with access to the River Thames for unloading coal.

With over 6,000 employees, the South Metropolitan Gas Company was second in the country only to the Gas, Light and Coke Company of North London.

In 1882 George became a director of the company, rising to Chairman in 1885. To increase efficiency, he adopted the principle of the sliding scales, whereby dividends and prices were linked. As prices fell, dividends were raised, and vice versa. In 1889 a profit-sharing scheme for the workmen was set up, followed in 1894 by a co-partnership scheme whereby all the workmen became share-holders. This culminated in the election by the workforce of two employee representatives to the board of directors. Over the next 60 years, most gas companies introduced similar schemes, contributing to improved labour relations.

The arrival of electricity in the 1880s was a threat to the gas industry. However, George was quick to implement new ideas and find new markets. In 1892 he was first to introduce free gas installation (for lighting and cooking) to homes previously not connected. This included installing pre-payment meters, giving payment security. The scheme was adopted throughout the country; gas for the working-classes had arrived.

George Livesey also found time for other activities. He served on the Council of the Institute of Civil Engineers from 1872-1908; he was a regular Sunday school teacher at Christ Church, Old Kent Road; he built the first free public library in Camberwell in 1890 (Livesey Library in Old Kent Road, now the Livesey Museum, opened 1974), and provided the land for Telegraph Hill Park (opened 1895) near New Cross. He was also a consultant and advisor to many other gas companies. His bronze statue (1910) by F W Pomeroy, formerly sited near the entrance to the gas works in Old Kent Road, is now at the Livesey Museum.

In 1859 George married Harriet Howard; they had no children. About 1878 they moved from their home at 147 Tulse Hill to a larger house, Penmaen, 50 Herne Hill, staying there until c1885. Penmaen was then demolished and Kestrel Avenue built over the site. The Liveseys moved to Tunbridge Wells and finally, c1895, to Shagbrook at Buckland near Reigate in Surrey. Here he died 4 October 1908. Over 7,000 gas workers attended his funeral at Nunhead Cemetery.

Following post-WW2 nationalisation, the South Metropolitan Gas Company became part of the South East Gas Board. Gas production was switched from coal to oil, and since the 1970s the supply has been from natural gas.

## John Locke (1805-80)
## 15 Herne Hill
## Legal Writer and Politician

John Locke Jr was the only son of John Locke (c1775-1853), a Southwark builder and surveyor. In the late 1820s, John senior moved to 15 Herne Hill (between Holmdene Avenue and Hollingbourne Road - now 93-99 Herne Hill) and lived there until his death. Educated in Dulwich and at Trinity College, Cambridge, John junior was called to the Bar at the Inner Temple in 1833, and joined the home circuit and Surrey sessions, where he also had a leading practice.

Between 1845 and 1857 he was one of the Common Pleaders of the City of London, after which he was appointed a QC. Locke became recorder of Brighton in 1861 and was elected as

Liberal MP for Southwark in April 1857, holding the seat until his death. As an MP, he was chiefly active on questions of local government and measures for improving the conditions of the working classes.

He married Laura Rosalie Cobb in 1847 and went to live at 22 Chester Street, Grosvenor Place. They had one son (John Henry Locke, b 1848). He was the author of a *Treatise on Game Law* (1836) which went through five editions, and *The Doctrine and Practice of Foreign Attachment in the Lord Mayor's Court* (1853).

About 1861, the family moved to 63 Eaton Place. In that year Locke introduced and saw passage through Parliament of a bill to allow witnesses in criminal cases the same right to substitute an affirmation for an oath, as applied in civil cases.

He died at 63 Eaton Place, 28 January 1880 and is buried in the catacombs at Norwood Cemetery.

## Sophie Crawford Lomas (c1847-1929) 51 Herne Hill Historian and Editor

Sophia (Sophie) was the daughter of W Crawford Williamson, Professor of Botany at Manchester Victoria University. Educated at Ellerslie School and College, Manchester, she began assisting her aunt, Mrs Everett Green, in calendaring Charles II's 'State Papers Domestic'. After Mrs Green's death in 1895, Sophie went on to complete work on the 'Addenda Papers' of Charles I. She continued to produce valuable work for the Public Record Office (PRO) for nearly 30 years.

In 1897 Sophie was asked to prepare a report on the manuscripts of Lord Egmont for the Historical Manuscripts Commission. As Inspector for the Commission, she published reports on the Earl of Ancaster, Earl of Denbigh, Marquis of Bath, Lord Montagu of Beaulieu, Sir George Wombwell, Sir John Graham of Fintry, G H Finch of Burley-on-the-Hill, Mrs Frankland-Russell-Astley, Mrs Barrett Lennard, the Duke of Portland, and many others.

In 1902 she was appointed Editor of Calendar of State Papers Foreign. While continuing her work for the Commission and the PRO, her new post took the greater part of her time. She edited Edwardian Inventories for County Huntingdon, Carlyle's Letters, the Papers of Oliver Cromwell, etc. She also brought out a new edition of Mrs Green's *Life of Princess Elizabeth Electress Palatine and Queen of Bohemia*, and collaborated with Sir Charles Firth on *Notes on the Diplomatic Relations between England and France.* For many years Sophie was a member of the Council of the

Royal Historical Society, for which she also edited documents.

Sophie married William Lomas (d 1915), son of George Lomas of Manchester and Southport. They had two daughters, Winifred (1869-1953) and Ethel Margaret (1873-1949). In 1922, the family moved from Sydenham to 51 Herne Hill, former home of Sax Rohmer.

Often working far into the night on her many projects, Sophie's health deteriorated. Having arranged and calendared the state papers of the reign of Elizabeth I to the eve of the Armada, illness forced her to hand the work to A H Hinds for completion.

Sophie died 17 April 1929, aged 81 and was buried in Norwood Cemetery. Her obituary in *The Times* noted the ample evidence of her ability in all her endeavours and spoke of "her generous nature and brilliant qualities." Her daughters, who never married, continued living at 51 Herne Hill.

## Alfred Longsdon (c1828-1893)
## 188 and 200 Denmark Hill
## Civil Engineer

From c1865 until his death Longsdon was the London representative for Krupps, the mighty German armaments manufacturer. Alfred Krupp (1812-87) founded the firm in 1837 and established one of the first Bessemer steel plants at his Essen factory in the Ruhr. Longsdon dealt with orders and queries from Britain and kept Krupps informed on British technology. He frequently answered comments and criticisms in the press on armaments issues. In 1888 he and Krupp's son, Friedrich Alfred Krupp (1854-1902), visited the Atlas Steel Works in Sheffield to view Atlas's gigantic new hydraulic forging press which could exert a force of over four tons. Krupp was so impressed that he instantly ordered one for the Essen works.

Alfred Longsdon was a younger brother of Robert Longsdon (c1825-72), Henry Bessemer's business partner, who was involved in steel manufacture using the Bessemer process. From c1865 Alfred Longsdon lived at 188 Denmark Hill, since demolished; 172 Denmark Hill now occupies the site. His next house, from c1880, was Fairfield, 200 Denmark Hill. This house, once also the home of Thomas Meller, is also now demolished. It was located opposite Henry Bessemer's house.

Alfred Longsdon died 27 November 1893. He is buried at Norwood Cemetery where his large, domed mausoleum is Grade II listed.

## Henry Dawson Lowry (1869-1906)
## 49 Dulwich Road
## Author

Henry, eldest son of Thomas Shaw Lowry and Winifred, née Dawson, was born in Truro 22 February 1869. Thomas later became bank manager at Camborne and moved the family there. Intended for the Wesleyan ministry, Henry attended Queen's College, Taunton, before becoming an unattached student at Oxford, graduating with honours in chemistry. The "delicate, nervous, romantic, high-strung, wilful and affectionate boy" wrote verse and played the piano. He contributed to the *Cornish Magazine* and was encouraged when W E Henley accepted his stories for the *National Observer* in 1891. Coming to London in 1893 and joining the group of 'Henley's young men', he wrote for that journal as long as Henley was editor.

Lowry also wrote for *Pall Mall Gazette*, joining the staff in 1895, and was on the staff of *B&W* (1895-98). In 1897 he became editor of *Ludgate Magazine* and a staff member of *Morning Post* the same year. Later he wrote as 'The Impenitent' in the *Daily Express* and contributed to other newspapers.

His first short story collections, *Wreckers and Methodists* (1893) and *Women's Tragedies* (1895) were well received. Subsequent books were: *A Man of Moods* (novel), *Make Believe*, *The Happy Exile*, *Strange Happenings* and *The First to Die*. Other works included *The City Halls of London: Stationers* and *The Valley of the Shadow*, a moving description of a cancer ward. A collection of poetry, *The Hundred Windows*, was published in 1904; and *A Dream of Daffodils - Last Poems* appeared posthumously in 1912. Lowry also wrote song lyrics for various composers. In the two decades after his death, several of his poems were set to music, one by Frank Bridge.

Literary critics judged Lowry's dramatic studies of country life in the Cornwall he knew and remembered the best of his output. "Refined, sympathetic and emotional," his work reflected "a fresh, vigorous and perceptive mind". His "tasteful verse" was noted for its "light and cheerful spirit."

H D Lowry lodged at 49 Dulwich Road, near Milton Road. No doubt his reputed devotion to the open air attracted him to nearby Brockwell Park. However, from 1898 increasing ill health cut his activities. His final years "were spent in pleasant retirement at Herne Hill, cheered by friendship and financial independence."

Unmarried, he had "some earnest friendships, as hundreds of letters, never to be published, go to prove." Described as being "warm hearted, impulsive and sociable... popular with colleagues and friends," Henry died of pneumonia and a wasting disease on 21 October 1906 aged 37. He is buried in Norwood Cemetery.

Curiously, H D Lowry features in a 1926 book by his cousin Catherine A Dawson Scott, *From Four Who are Dead*. Purporting to be communications from beyond the grave, it has him drawn to eastern art and life, speculating on reincarnation, feeling "content to be in the tides of life and time ...." In 1927, Mrs Scott published Lowry's unfinished novel, *Wheal Darkness*.

## Connie Lupino (1892-1959) 33 Ardbeg Road Dancer

Constance Gladys O'Shea, youngest of five girls in an Irish theatrical family, was born in Camberwell and raised in Liverpool.

From childhood she performed as one of the 'Sisters Emerald'.

Touring the world to great acclaim, she was once billed "the fastest tap dancer alive". Petite, blue-eyed Connie Emerald met Stanley Lupino in 1914 when they co-starred in *Go to Jericho*. At that time she was sole support of her large family. The couple were soon engaged, and married in summer 1915. Their fortunes improved; and they moved to 33 Ardbeg Road in 1917.

When in 1926 Stanley and Connie were hired for a Broadway operetta, *Naughty Riquette*, their daughters, Ida and Rita (b 1920) were sent to a boarding school in Brighton, where Connie's sister, Nell O'Shea, had her own film studio. The couple returned to England before a further Broadway success in 1927, coming home again later that year.

In 1933 and again in 1934 Connie accompanied Ida to America, to look after her in Hollywood at the film studios. Warm and friendly, Connie endeared herself to all. She would entertain friends with a tap routine to her theme song 'Tea for Two'; and she taught Ida's young circle the Lambeth Walk, the dance made famous by Stanley's cousin Lupino Lane. Connie also joined a bridge club and tap-danced daily to keep fit. Screenwriter Malvin Wald called her "a very lovely woman" and Errol Flynn, whom she loved like a son, dubbed her "Connetta Moonstone."

Connie and her daughters were very close; Ida listened to her as to no one else. Proud of the Lupino/O'Shea theatrical heritage, she desperately wanted a grandchild to continue the family line. Not wishing to be a burdensome mother-in-law, however, she moved to Las Vegas, where she had friends; Ida bought an apartment building for her there.

On Christmas Eve 1959, being driven by her boyfriend, professional gambler Alfred Quoback, to spend the holidays with her family, she was injured in a car crash. Connie died two days later.

## Ida Lupino (1918-95)
## 33 Ardbeg Road
## Actress and Director

Ida Lupino was born in 33 Ardbeg Road at the height of an air raid, 4 February 1918. Taught singing, music and drawing by her grandfather George Hook Lupino Jr, Ida performed from early childhood, also writing plays and skits. Her father, Stanley, coached her and sister Rita in acting and stagecraft. At 13 Ida entered RADA, where G B Shaw cast her in *Heartbreak House*. This led to her film debut, aged 15, in *Her First Affair*. Five other British films rapidly followed. In August 1933, accompanied by her mother Connie, she sailed to America, on contract with Paramount. Her first Hollywood film was *Search for Beauty*. However, before starting her third film, a bout of polio nearly ended her career. Recovered, she made eleven more films before leaving Paramount and shedding her dyed-blonde image.

From 1939 she established herself in serious roles in major films, notably *The Light That Failed*, of which the *New York Times* said "A little ingénue suddenly burst forth as a great actress." Now signed with Warner Bros., she gave outstanding performances in *They Drive by Night*, *High Sierra*, *The Sea Wolf* and *Ladies in Retirement*. She won the New York Film Critics Award for *The Hard Way* (1942). That year, with gasoline rationing about to begin, Ida, Connie and Rita shared a house near the studios and started a Victory Garden. Ida made war effort films, including

*Hollywood Canteen*, about the club, of which she was a regular supporter, where servicemen met the stars.

Her marriage to actor Louis Hayward ended in 1945 after seven years. In 1948 she became an American citizen and married film writer and producer Collier Young, with whom she founded a production company. She wrote and co-produced *Not Wanted* (1949), and took over from the director, Elmer Clifton, when he fell ill. She went on to write and direct seven further films with such challenging themes as unwed mothers, rape and bigamy. Her astute casting gave several young actors their first break; and her pioneering, highly regarded work opened a door for women directors.

Ida's creative endeavours included writing short stories and children's books and composing music. She won a *Holiday* magazine award for artistic courage; and the Foreign Press Association named her 'Woman of the Year'. In 1951 she divorced Young (though they remained friends and collaborators) and married actor Howard Duff, with whom she had a daughter, Bridget, in 1952. Interrupting Ida's film career, the Duffs co-starred in a TV comedy series, *Mr Adams and Eve*. Ida made many other TV appearances until the late 1970s and directed numerous programmes. Cast in *Junior Bonner* (1972) with Steve McQueen, she continued making films until 1978. Having won a Masquers award for excellence, an Emmy nomination and other honours, she received an Artistry in Cinema Award in 1979.

The Duffs' turbulent marriage ended in 1984. Ida's health later declined, and she died on 3 August 1995 following a stroke. *The Times* called her "one of the outstanding film actresses of her generation...in her element playing tough tarts in hard-boiled yarns... where her sultry good looks made her a perfect foil to actors such as Humphrey Bogart and George Raft." The most famous of the theatrical Lupinos, she epitomised what Edward VII had once dubbed "the royal family of greasepaint."

## Stanley Lupino (1893-1942)
## 33 Ardbeg Road
## Musical Comedy Star

Stanley Richard Lupino-Hook traced his heritage to Georgio Luppino, a nobleman turned puppeteer, born in Bologna in 1612. Stanley was born 15 May 1893 in a hansom cab that his mother, ballerina Florence Ann Webster, had taken after shopping in Petticoat Lane. Five years later Florence died aged 39 and the family home in Kennington Road was repossessed. Stanley joined his father's troupe, making his debut aged six in *King Klondyke*. By age 21 he was a headliner in musicals and Drury Lane pantomimes.

In 1917 he and his wife Connie, whom he had married two years earlier, moved to 33 Ardbeg Road. He starred in the musical *Suzette*, the operetta

*Arlette* and as Widow Twankey in *Aladdin* during this period. Other musical hits included *Dover Street to Dixie*, which ran for 108 performances in 1923, and *Better Days* which had 135 performances at the Hippodrome in 1925, and featured Stanley singing 'Could Lloyd George Do It?'

At 5' 6" (1.68m) tall, with jet black hair, a warm smile and huge, luminous eyes, Stanley became England's best known comedian. Keen to continue the family legacy into the 12th generation, he taught his daughters acting skills, built a theatre for them and formed a 'Little Company' with their cousins to rehearse and perform. In 1930 the family moved from Ardbeg Road to a mansion, formerly called Holmdene, at 60 Leigham Court Road, Streatham (later renumbered 152).

In the 1930s Stanley wrote a novel, *Crazy Days*, and made several musical films, including *Love Lies*, *Facing the Music* and *Honeymoon for Three*, while continuing his stage career. He also wrote or co-authored some of his scripts and screenplays. With his wife now away in Hollywood chaperoning their daughter Ida, he fell in love with his new co-star, the actress Sally Gray (b 1916). However, he and Connie never divorced.

During WW2, Stanley was an Air Raids Precautions Warden. Though diagnosed with cancer, he continued his duties, while also writing and starring in *Lady Behave*, the first major musical to open in London after the war began. However, in September 1941 he was forced to quit to undergo a major operation. Though unable to perform again, he wrote a stage drama, *The Love Racket*, before his death on 10 June 1942. He was buried in Lambeth Cemetery near his brother Mark and his idol, the comedian Dan Leno. Stanley left £62,312, his Streatham house and personal possessions; the proceeds of a £10,000 insurance policy went to Sally Gray. The house, however, was in the path of Nazi bombers making nightly raids on Croydon Airfield, and was severely damaged on 1 August 1944.

Stanley Lupino's periodic projects to work with daughter Ida were never realised; and his hopes for the dynasty were to be thwarted when grand-daughter Bridget decided against an acting career.

Daughter Rita joined Connie and Ida in Hollywood c1938. A superb dancer, she appeared at the Coconut Grove and in four films in the 1940s. Ida tried to advance her sister's career, coaching her for a screen test and later casting her in three films in 1949-50. Rita achieved great success as a dancer, including performances at New York's Carnegie Hall. She made a further film in 1970 and had occasional featured roles on television from 1959-76. At the time of writing (2006), she is living in retirement, the last of the Herne Hill Lupinos.

## Sir John Maitland, Bart (1879-1949) 62 Holmdene Avenue Teacher

Born 25 November 1879 in Kensington, John Maitland was educated at Halleybury School and at Trinity College, Cambridge, where he studied law. He was called to the bar in 1903, but preferred teaching. For some years he taught in preparatory schools, first at Broadstairs and later at Hemel Hempstead.

During WW1 he served as a Lieutenant in the Royal Garrison Artillery and was mentioned in dispatches. In 1915 he married Kathleen Offley, née Keates (d 1959); they had one daughter. In 1920 he was appointed Assistant Master at Alleyn's School in Dulwich, remaining in that post until he retired. From c1921 until his death he lived at 62 Holmdene Avenue. Sir John Maitland died 27 November 1949, at Ulverston in the Lake District.

***Maitland Coat of Arms***

John Maitland succeeded his father, Sir John Nisbet Maitland (1850-1936), to become the 6th Baronet. In 1949 the title passed to his younger brother, George Ramsay Maitland (1882-1960).

## Roddy McDowall (1928-98) 204 Herne Hill Road Actor

Roderick Andrew Anthony Jude McDowall was born at 204 Herne Hill Road 17 September 1928. His parents, merchant seaman Thomas Andrew and Wensfriede L Corcoran McDowall, and his sister Virginia (b 1927), had moved there earlier that year. Young Roddy studied at St Josephs College, Beulah Hill and at the Hanover Academy of Dramatic Art, displaying precocious acting talent early on.

Beginning with *Scruffy* and *Murder in the Family* at the age of nine, Roddy made 17 films in UK between 1938-40, including *Yellow Sands* and *Just William*. Evacuated to America and moving to Hollywood, he became an international child star in *How Green Was My Valley*, followed by *On the Sunny Side*, *My Friend Flicka* and *Lassie Come Home*. One adult part was as Malcolm in Orson Welles' 1948 *Macbeth*. Roddy loved his early career, but later wearied of being typecast into his late twenties as the fresh-faced English youth. To expand his range he took a variety of stage and television roles in New York, winning both a Broadway Tony award and a TV Emmy in 1960.

Returning to films, he played character parts, notably as Octavian in *Cleopatra* with childhood co-star and friend Elizabeth Taylor. In 1968 he achieved renewed fame as Cornelius, the wise simian, in *Planet of the Apes*. He recreated the role in most of the

sequels, and starred in the popular television spin-off. Though other films followed, including *Poseidon Adventure* and *Funny Lady*, he had become identified with, and will probably best be remembered for the ape role. In all, he made some 140 films.

A talented photographer, he built a parallel career with photo-features of celebrities in glossy magazines, and produced two books of photographs. A good friend and confidant to many, Roddy McDowall was discreet about his homosexuality and was never goaded into a Hollywood marriage. He died in Los Angeles of lung cancer 3 October 1998; his ashes were scattered at sea. The Academy of Motion Picture Arts and Sciences renamed its photographic archive in his memory.

## Sir Henry McDowell (1910-2000)
## 2 Donne Court, Burbage Road
## Rhodesian Civil Servant

Born 10 December 1910 in Johannesburg, Henry McLorinan McDowell was educated at Witwatersrand University, South Africa, at Queen's College, Oxford and at Yale University. During WW2, he served in East Africa and in South East Asia, in the Northern Rhodesia Regiment.

Henry joined the Colonial Service in 1938 as a District Officer in Northern Rhodesia (now Zambia). From 1953, he was a member of the Economic and Financial Working Party that helped form the Federation of Rhodesia and Nyasaland. He joined the Federal Civil Service, becoming Secretary of Transport in 1955 and later Secretary to the Treasury. Committed to the cause of multiracialism, Henry was disappointed by the Federation's dissolution, but gracefully played his part in achieving it. He received his knighthood in the Dissolution Honours of 1964.

In 1965, Ian Smith (b 1919), the Prime Minister of Southern Rhodesia, made a Unilateral Declaration of Independence (UDI) from Britain, creating a Rhodesian State under white minority rule. Sir Humphrey Gibbs, the Governor of Southern Rhodesia, insisted that, as the representative of the monarch, he was the legitimate authority in the colony. At that time, Sir Henry was a loyal supporter and confidant of the beleaguered Gibbs and would have been his successor had Gibbs died or become incapacitated. Gibbs retired as Governor in 1969 when Smith broke all remaining links with Britain. Majority rule eventually came with the formation of Zimbabwe in 1979.

Sir Henry served on the board of many companies in Rhodesia and later Zimbabwe, including Chairman (1969-79) of the local board of Barclays International. From 1971-81 he was

Chancellor of the University of Rhodesia, a multiracial institution, and during that difficult time succeeded in preserving its traditions with dignity and integrity.

From c1980, Sir Henry lived at 2 Donne Court, Burbage Road. He died 10 May 2000. His wife Norah predeceased him in 1995.

## Thomas William Meller (c1770-1850) 200 Denmark Hill Coach Builder

Thomas Meller's main claim to fame is the location of his tomb - in St Paul's Cathedral churchyard, next to the Paul's Cross memorial - where hundreds of Londoners and tourists pass by every day. The inscription reads:-

IN MEMORY OF
THOMAS WILLIAM MELLER, ESQ.
OF DENMARK HILL SURREY
WHO DIED 8 APRIL 1850
AGED 80 YEARS

In his will, he had requested "to be laid in the vault of my late mother and my infant child in St Paul's [Cathedral] churchyard."

Thomas Meller lived at 200 Denmark Hill from the 1810s until his death. The house, later called Fairfield, was demolished in the early 1900s. It was located between Rutland Court and Deepdene Road.

Thomas Meller's coach works were based in Southwark at Blackfriars Road (then known as Great Surrey Street). However, his name disappeared from the trade directories after c1820. His will lists numerous properties, many in the Blackfriars Road area, suggesting that he had retired from business and lived on the income from these. He had two sons: the elder, Thomas William Meller (1808-71), took holy orders and became Rector of Woodbridge in Suffolk; and the younger, Walter Meller, also became a coach builder.

## Walter Meller (1819-86) 200 Denmark Hill Member of Parliament

The younger son of Thomas William Meller, Walter Meller is listed in the 1841 census as a coach builder, aged 20. Born and brought up at 200 Denmark Hill, he was christened on 16 February 1819 at Christ Church, Blackfriars Road, Southwark. In 1845 he married Elizabeth, the daughter of Thomas Peters of the Grange, Kilburn and for a few years the couple lived at Kilburn. In the 1853 Kelly's directory he is listed under "Wyburn, Meller and Turner, coach makers to Her Majesty the late Queen Dowager, 121 Long Acre and 9 Park Lane." From the 1850s until his death, Walter lived in a large mansion, Broadlands, on the west side of Clapham Common, on a site now next to Broomfield Road.

In the 1860s Walter was made Captain Commandant of the Surrey Light Horse Volunteers, and later Hon. Colonel of the 4th Tower Hamlets Rifle Volunteers. In 1865 he was elected as Conservative MP for Stafford, then re-elected in 1868. However, he was unseated on petition in 1869. He became a Magistrate and Deputy-Lieutenant for Middlesex, and Deputy-Lieutenant of the Tower.

At the time of the 1881 census, Walter Meller was living at 3 Brunswick Terrace, Hove, Sussex, while his wife and youngest daughter still lived at Broadlands. He died there on 10 January 1886, leaving £46,746 in his will.

## Ralph Merrifield (1913-95)
## 32 Poplar Walk
## Archaeologist and Curator

Ralph Merrifield was born 22 August 1913 in north west London. His father was a railway official, his mother a junior school teacher. After his father's early death Ralph went to Brighton, where his first job was at the Brighton Museum. There he collected and labelled wild flowers for the Children's Department; handled archaeological material brought in from digs; sorted and arranged a large collection of anthropological items, and arranged exhibitions. He also took part in archaeological digs himself.

As an external student he matriculated at Brighton Technical College in 1929. In 1932 he took the Intermediate Examination of London University and in 1935 was awarded the external BA Diploma. WW2, however, upset his plans. He joined the RAF and became an Intelligence Officer, and was sent to train in photographic identification, serving in India and Indonesia.

Ralph returned to the Brighton Museum until 1950, when he was appointed Curator of the Guildhall Museum in the City of London. Also in that year he was elected a Fellow of the Society of Antiquaries. In 1951 he married Lysbeth Webb, a colleague at the Guildhall Museum, and moved from Brighton to London. The family went to live at 32 Poplar Walk in 1969.

Ralph's travels included to Ghana in 1956 to arrange the new National Museum, and in 1973 to various Japanese cities with an exhibition of the history of the river Thames. In 1975 the Guildhall Museum amalgamated with the London Museum to form the Museum of London; and Ralph was put in charge of the Prehistoric and Roman Departments.

Ralph lectured extensively on Roman London and published three books on the subject, including in 1965, *The Roman City of London*, a landmark in the study of the city. He spent the last two years before his retirement as the Museum of London's Deputy Director. When Ralph retired a Festschrift (a collection of essays or articles in honour of a distinguished scholar) was published to celebrate his life and work. In 1979 he was awarded a Jubilee Medal; and in 1989 an Honorary Doctorate was conferred on him by the University of London.

After his retirement Ralph did a great deal of lecturing. He also had the time to write the book he had long wanted to complete on the archaeology of ritual and magic. In 1994 Ralph delivered the Hugh Chapman Memorial lecture in memory of a much loved colleague who tragically died young.

Ralph died 9 January 1995. He has been described as the most distinguished scholar to have served on the Museum's staff.

## Freddie Mills (1919-65)
## 186 Denmark Hill
## Boxer

Born 26 June 1919 in 7 Terrace Road, the poorest street in Bournemouth, Frederick Percival (Freddie) Mills received his first pair of boxing gloves on his eleventh birthday, and would regularly spar with his older brother Charlie.

Freddie left school aged 14 and began work as an apprentice milkman. His first boxing match took place on 2 February 1936 at Bournemouth's Westover Ice Rink. He won by a knockout in the first round. Shortly after, he was signed up by promoter Bob Turner, and began boxing full time at fairground booths and South Coast venues. He boxed for 'nobbins', the coins spectators threw into the ring after a fight. Three pounds was considered a good night's earnings.

By the end of 1940, Freddie Mills had had 58 professional fights, of which he won 46. His boxing style was characterised by two-fisted aggression, powerful left hooks, ability to take punishment, tenacity and great courage.

After being called up into the RAF during WW2, Freddie became a PT instructor. He was allowed time off to box professionally. In August 1940 he hitch-hiked to Liverpool to fight the British middleweight champion Jack McAvoy. A clear victory put him firmly into the big league.Shortly afterwards, Ted Broadribb, the well known boxing promoter, became his manager.

After service in India he left the RAF, and in May 1946 fought Gus Lesnevich at Harringay Arena. He took severe punishment and the fight was stopped in the tenth round. However, in July 1948, he won a rematch at White City and became world light-heavyweight boxing champion.

Later that year, Freddie married Chrissie, his manager's daughter and ex-wife of boxer Donald McCorkindale. Their wedding took place at Herne Hill Methodist Church and they moved to 186 Denmark Hill. There they lived with their two daughters and Chrissie's son from her previous marriage.

In January 1950 Freddie was knocked out in the tenth round, while defending his world light-heavyweight title against American Joey Maxim at Earls Court. Prompting from Chrissie led to him retiring from the ring; and he never fought again.

In retirement he occupied himself with a second career as a popular light entertainer making frequent television appearances; and following his business interests including boxing

promotion. He became well known as 'Celebrity Freddie' and was respected for his charity work. A keen family man, he enjoyed spending time at their large, comfortable house in Denmark Hill, complete with swimming pool.

Freddie opened Freddie Mills' Chinese Restaurant in Charing Cross Road, later converting it into a nightclub, Freddie Mills' Nite Spot. Unfortunately the nightclub was not a success. Freddie died in Middlesex Hospital 25 July 1965 after sustaining a gunshot wound to the head. He had apparently been resting in his car, parked in Goslett Yard behind his nightclub. He is buried in Camberwell New Cemetery.

The inquest verdict on his death was suicide, a finding which has been strongly contested, not least by his wife, Chrissie. However, it has never been established whether he committed suicide or was murdered as a result of gangland protection rackets which were rife in the West End at the time. In his will he left £3,767.

## Prof. Eric Mottram (1924-95)
## 40 Guernsey Grove
## Poet and Academic

Eric Noel William Mottram was born in London 29 December 1924. After wartime naval service and a first class Cambridge degree, he taught in Zürich, Singapore and Holland. In 1961 he was appointed Lecturer in American Literature at King's College London. This was the first such post in Britain.

In 1963 he co-founded London University's Institute of United States Studies, the first of its kind in the country. He was later appointed Emeritus Professor of English and American Literature at King's College London.

Eric was well known for his pioneering work on the Beat writers and on post-WW2 American poetry. His work also included studies on guns and cars in American culture, the fears of invasion in American society, 1960s rock culture, and the music of John Cage. In addition, he wrote widely on many other 19th and 20th century American authors, and on other aspects of modern American culture.

Eric was himself an accomplished poet, being one of the moving forces behind the 1960s 'British poetry revival'. He published over 20 books of poetry, over 200 articles, and several books and pamphlets of literary and cultural criticism. He also made an important contribution as a teacher and educator.

His extensive archive of some 12,000 books, hundreds of boxes of papers, several hundred audio tapes and other materials, 'The Mottram Collection', is now housed at King's College. Eric Mottram moved into 40 Guernsey Grove c1973 and stayed there until his death on 16 January 1995.

## Sir Richard Muir (1857-1924) 5 Cosbycote Avenue and 99 Herne Hill Barrister

Born the son of a Greenock ship broker, Richard David Muir came to London with the ambition of becoming an actor. After working as a parliamentary reporter for *The Times*, he changed his mind and turned instead to the law.

He is widely regarded as the greatest Crown prosecutor of his time, and was engaged in almost every Old Bailey trial of note from about 1901 until his death. Amongst the most famous and successful cases he prosecuted were the Crippen trial in 1910 and that of the Stratton brothers, Alfred and Albert in 1905.

Dr Hawley Harvey Crippen had murdered his actress wife, Cora, buried her dismembered body in the cellar of their Holloway home, and fled to America with his mistress, Ethel le Neve. When brought back to London and in custody, upon learning that his prosecuting counsel was to be Richard Muir, Crippen remarked "I wish it had been anybody else... I fear the worst". In court, Muir interrogated Crippen for three hours, revealing his lies and evasions. Found guilty, Crippen was later hanged at Pentonville prison.

The Stratton murder case was the first in which fingerprint evidence was used to obtain a conviction. Albert and Alfred Stratton were hanged for the murder of Deptford shopkeeper Thomas Farrow and his wife Ann. Crucial to the case was Albert's thumb print on a cash box found at the scene. Having studied the subject of fingerprinting, Muir, who was known for his skilful use of physical evidence, knowledgeably questioned many expert witnesses and obtained a conviction.

Devoting his career to the criminal bar, Muir worked through many nights preparing his cases until they were foolproof. He was well known for his 'playing cards' which were small cards containing his coloured notes and evidence. One colour would be for direct examination, another for cross-examination, and so on. Feared by his clerks and officers from Scotland Yard, Muir asked of them such high standards as he expected from himself.

Muir became Senior Treasury Counsel in 1908. He was later appointed Recorder of Colchester by the then Home Secretary, Winston Churchill, as a reward for his work on the Mylius case. Edward Mylius had claimed that Prince George, later King George V, had married in Malta in 1890. Muir successfully obtained a conviction for criminal libel. Other famous trials included two further libel cases, those involving Lord Alfred Douglas, the associate of Oscar Wilde.

Muir was a Master of the Bench of the Middle Temple. A knighthood was conferred on him in 1918. But he was heartbroken when his only son, also a barrister, died of influenza in the same year whilst serving in France during WW1.

Richard Muir married Mary Beatrice Leycester; they lived at 5 Cosbycote Avenue from 1894-98. They moved to 99 Herne Hill (then numbered 15a) in 1898, when the house had just been built, living there until c1915. The house is now an osteopath's surgery, F W Bruggemeyer. Muir died 14 January 1924 in his house in Camden House Court, Kensington and is buried in Norwood Cemetery.

### Sam Mussabini (1867-1927)
### 84 Burbage Road
### Sports Coach

Scipio Augustus (Sam) Mussabini was born in Lewisham 11 March 1867, but lived at 84 Burbage Road from 1913 until his death in 1927. He was the fourth of six children of Neocles Gaspard Mussabini (1827-1915), a diplomat, war correspondent, journalist and author, and his wife Aline (c1840-1911).

As a young man Sam had a strong interest in athletics, football and cricket, and developed into a competent athlete. He made a successful career as a newspaper columnist, publisher and author, writing on sports and billiards, and as an athletics and cycling coach. He is particularly famous for coaching the sprinter Harold Abrahams, who won the 100 metres gold medal and a silver medal in the 4 x 100 metre relay at the 1924 Paris Olympic Games. This success was relived in the popular 1981 Oscar-winning film *Chariots of Fire*, where Sam was memorably played by the actor Ian Holm. In 1885 when he was 18, Sam married Emma Nichols (1866-1961), a farmer's daughter from Hove. They had three sons and four daughters.

One of the main reasons for Sam Mussabini's success as a coach was his 'scientific' approach to training. He developed his techniques by observing and learning from professional athletes and incorporating the results of this research into his training methods. He also used photography to study his athletes in action. Sam describes this application of new technology in his 1913 book *The Complete Athletic Trainer*. Although proven successful, as a paid coach in an amateur era his methods met with opposition from the sporting establishment. One of his earliest achievements was at the Herne Hill Stadium where in 1894 he helped Bert Harris of the Polytechnic Cycling Club to win the first professional one-mile national championships. Following this success he was appointed trainer to the Dunlop Cycle Pacing Team, also based at Herne Hill Stadium; and in 1913 he was employed as Senior Coach by the Polytechnic Harriers.

In the twenty years between 1908 and 1928, athletes trained by Sam won a total of five gold, two silver and four bronze Olympic medals. He also achieved recognition as a leading billiards referee, adjudicating at many top-class billiards matches and publishing four books on the subject.

Sam's final years were marred by illness. In 1927 he had gone to Nice to convalesce. However, returning home for his 60th birthday, he died in his sleep on 25 March at Etaples station, near Calais. He was buried in Hampstead Cemetery in the family grave.

## Lesslie Newbigin (1909-98)
## 89-91 Stradella Road
## Missionary and Theologian

Born 8 December 1909 in Newcastle-upon-Tyne, the son of a shipping merchant, James Edward Lesslie Newbigin was educated at the Quakers' Leighton School, Reading and at Queen's College, Cambridge. He studied geography and economics with the intention of joining his father's shipping company, but became caught up in the Student Christian Movement (SCM). After graduation in 1931 he became secretary of the Scottish SCM where he first met Helen Henderson, whom he married in 1936.

In 1936 Lesslie Newbigin was ordained and posted as District Missionary to Madras in South India where he became a fluent Tamil speaker. There he was drawn into the discussions aimed towards uniting the Presbyterian/Congregational, Methodist and Anglican churches. At the inauguration of the united Church of South India in 1947, he became one of the 14 new bishops consecrated. Lesslie was appointed as Bishop of Madurai and Ramnad, in Tamil Nadu. His book, *The Reunion of the Church* (1948), described his ideas on church unity in South India. However, at the 1958 Lambeth Conference, his views were to clash with those of Geoffrey Fisher (1887-1972), the Archbishop of Canterbury.

During the 1950s, air travel made it possible for him to attend key meetings of the World Council of Churches (WCC) and the International Missionary Council (IMC), as a delegate of the Church of South India. In 1959 he reluctantly took the post of General Secretary of the IMC, by then drawing close to integration with the WCC. In 1961 he was made Associate General Secretary of the WCC. However, his love of India made it easy for him to accept the post of Bishop of Madras in 1965.

Newbigin retired as Bishop in 1974, receiving a CBE, and took work as a lecturer in theology at Selly Oak College, Birmingham. He served as Moderator of the General Assembly of the United Reform Church (1978-79), and from 1980-88 as minister of a small congregation at Winson Green, Birmingham. He lived at the Abbeyfield Home, 89-91 Stradella Road, from c1992 until his death on 30 January 1998 and was cremated at Norwood Cemetery. His wife, who died in 1999, was survived by a son and three daughters.

## Edward Chambers Nicholson (1827-90)
## 5 Herne Hill
## Chemist and Dye Manufacturer

Edward Chambers Nicholson was born in Lincoln in January 1827. Aged ten he was sent to school in Uxbridge, Middlesex. He then started work assisting a chemist and druggist in Andover, Hampshire. Later he moved to a laboratory in London, and in 1845 enrolled as one of the first students at the Royal College of Chemistry.

After five years at the College, two of which he worked as a research assistant, Edward joined a South Wales company to investigate the chemistry of iron making. He later moved to Aberdare, Scotland. There he contracted typhoid fever, forcing a return to London. In 1853, having recovered, he set up a chemical manufacturing company (Simpson, Maule and Nicholson), based in Walworth in partnership with two former fellow college students. Nicholson led their research and development work, successfully transforming the results into viable manufacturing processes. It was said that "in him was united the genius of the manufacturer and the habits of a scientific investigator". One of his most important discoveries was a method of making magenta dye. By 1865 they were the largest producers of coal tar colours in Britain. The original premises in Walworth had by now become too small, and in the same year they moved to the new purpose-built Atlas Dye Works at Hackney Wick.

A number of other companies began using Nicholson's magenta dye process and he decided to sue. Unfortunately his patents were badly drafted, and after three years of long and costly litigation, a House of Lords judgement declared that they were invalid. Others could then to go ahead with magenta dye manufacture, the resulting competition bringing about a 95% collapse in dye prices. In 1868, when only 41 but already a very rich man, Edward decided to retire from the business. However, he continued his research work and obtained a number of additional patents - the last in 1870.

On his retirement, Edward moved to the former home of Elhanan Bicknell, 5 Herne Hill, which he named Carlton House. Here he lived until his death on 23 October 1890. He was survived by his wife Louisa and son John, both of whom continued to live in the house for another eight years. The house was later demolished.

### William Henry Noon (1860-1932)
### 220 Croxted Road
### Restaurateur

William Henry Noon was born in Kingsland, Hackney. He initially followed his father into bookbinding. However, preferring a more lucrative trade, he opened a coffee room in Homerton High Street and later a dining room for cabbies at 2 High St, Bloomsbury. In 1901 William was living with his wife Annie and their family at 67 Croxted Road. He had already opened a second dining room at 2 Pemberton Row (near Johnson's Court off Fleet Street).

By 1908 the Noons had moved to 220 Croxted Road, living there until 1912, when they went to 138 Upper Tulse Hill.

William Noon opened his last and flagship restaurant at 69 High Holborn. It served three-course businessman's lunches for 1/6d (7½p). There were waitresses in black and white uniforms, snow white tablecloths; and the diners sat on black leather settles. One satisfied customer dedicated this poem to 'the Proprietor of the Holborn restaurant':

> Noon, noon, glorious noon,
>
> Punctual, but never one moment too soon,
>
> Since early morning when we broke our fast
>
> We've been wishing for noon and the midday repast.
>
> Twelve o'clock comes, what a blessing and boon
>
> What would the day be, were there not Mr Noon?
>
> God bless the man, be he saint be he sinner
>
> Who thought to associate Noon and our dinner.

The Bloomsbury and Holborn restaurants carried on into the 1930s, by which time William had left Tulse Hill for rural Oxshott.

When he died on 13 October 1932, his estate was valued at £16,836, proving he was right to leave bookbinding.

## Marian Nowakowski (1912-2000)
## 97 Herne Hill
## Opera Singer

Born of Polish parents at Herten, Germany, 3 August 1912, Marian Zygmunt Nowakowski studied with the great Adam Didur at Lvov Conservatory. Making his debut with the Lvov Opera in 1937, he escaped when the Nazis invaded, becoming a Lieutenant in the émigré Polish Army in Scotland. As a soloist with the Polish Army Choir, based at the Carnegie Dunfermline Trust's Music Institute, he gave concerts all over Britain, including hospitals and military camps.

Nowakowski's first London solo appearance was in *The Messiah* at the Royal Albert Hall in 1944. He made many recordings as Marian Zygmunt. One, *An Eriskay Love Lilt*, was chosen by the then Princess Elizabeth as a favourite on *Records I Like* for BBC Radio in 1947. That year, Nowakowski also made his Covent Garden debut in *Il Travatore*. As principal bass he sang 20 major roles at the Royal Opera

House from 1947-57, notably Boris Godunov, Sarastro (*The Magic Flute*) and Ramfis (*Aida*). He sang Mephistopheles (*Faust*) and Sparafucile (*Rigoletto*) for Welsh National Opera in 1959 and the Hermit (*Der Freichutz*) at Sadler's Wells, 1963.

During this period he recorded under Beecham, Barbirolli, Boult and Sargent, worked for Radio Free Europe and gave charity concerts in support of central European countries. Though his Royal Opera contract prevented his accepting invitations from the Vienna State Opera and the Met, he occasionally sang oratorio abroad, notably *The Dream of Gerontius* in Rome, 1957.

From 1964 Nowakowski taught voice and opera production at the Royal College of Music in Kingston, Jamaica. There he encouraged pupil Willard White to pursue an opera career. He also taught at the University of Southern Mississippi. Returning to London in 1977, he moved with his wife to the house at 97 Herne Hill which was to be his home for the rest of his life. He continued to perform occasionally, including two concerts in Dunfermline, and to teach privately.

Nowakowski had married Julia Demska while still in Poland. They were reunited after WW2 when she recognised his voice on a radio broadcast from London. They had four daughters. In Julia's later years she was paralysed and unable to speak; he looked after her in their home in Herne Hill. Then osteoarthritis bent his once imposing figure; but his rich, mellow voice remained, even into his 80s. Nowakowski's last public appearance was a survey of his career at the Carnegie Library, Herne Hill. He died on 4 April 2000.

## Wilfred George Oakley (1905-98)
## 12 Courtmead Close
## Physician

Wilfred Oakley, MD, FRCP, was born 23 August 1905, the son of Rev. Canon G D Oakley, who at the time was Vicar of St Polycarp's Church in Everton, Liverpool.

Educated at Gonville and Caius College, Cambridge and at St Bartholomew's Hospital, Wilfred was awarded his MD in 1934 and became an FRCP in 1942. In his second week as a medical student he met Hemione Violet Wingate-Saul (d 1993), whom he married in 1931.

Whilst at St Bartholomew's, Wilfred developed an interest in diabetes, to which he devoted his professional career. In 1938 he moved to King's College Hospital's Diabetic Department, which he headed from 1957 to 1970. Under his direction the Department flourished in terms of patient care, teaching, and research.

Thanks in large part to Wilfrid's work, an eight-fold reduction in the perinatal mortality of pregnant women with diabetes was achieved. He collaborated on two textbooks, contributed to many others and published many scientific papers on diabetes. Always a hard worker, Wilfred gave up private practice only when he reached his 82nd birthday.

Wilfred moved to 12 Courtmead Close, Burbage Road in around 1993/4 and lived there until his death on Christmas Day, 1998.

## Richard Hotham Pigeon (1789-1851) 216 Denmark Hill Treasurer of Christ's Hospital

After his education at Dr Willett's Academy in Brixton, Pigeon was apprenticed in 1805 to Fynmore and Palmer, wholesale druggists of 31 Throgmorten Street in the City of London; by 1812 he had become a partner in the firm. From 1841-50 he was the first Treasurer of the Pharmaceutical Society. He married Elizabeth Toulmin (1793-1854) and they had a son and two daughters.

From 1835-47, Pigeon was Treasurer of Christ's Hospital, the school for boys in Newgate Street in the City of London, founded in 1553 for orphans. It was also known as the Blue Coat School, from its uniform. In those days, the role of Treasurer was equivalent to a chief executive's job now, and included overseeing the work of the headmaster. The Treasurer had his own separate house on the premises. While in office, Pigeon is reported to have made great improvements in the school's administration. In 1902 the school moved to Horsham and the General Post Office was built on the former site. The girls' school had moved to Hertford in 1704.

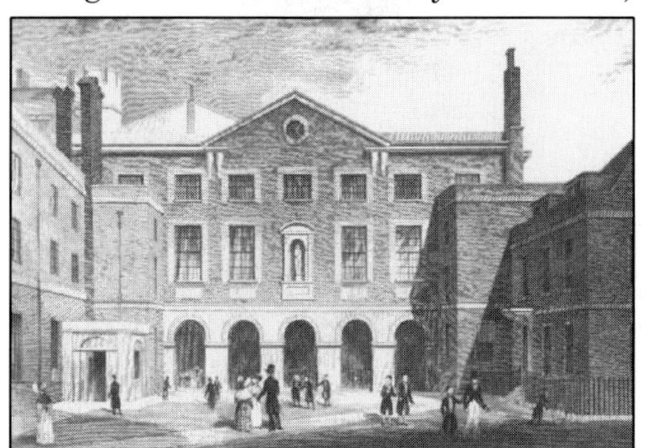

*Christ's Hospital c1830*

About 1850, Pigeon moved to 216 Denmark Hill. The house was demolished in the early 1900s; the site is now occupied by numbers 230 and 232, built in the 1920s. He died there on 10 June 1851 aged 62 and is buried in the catacombs at Norwood Cemetery. About 1840, his druggist business had been renamed Richard H Pigeon & Son. However, in 1852, only a year after his father's death, the son died and the firm was wound up.

## Sidney Pike (1858 - 1923) 35 Herne Hill Road Artist

Sidney Pike, a painter of landscapes and rural subjects, was born in Lambeth in March 1858. His parents were Mestach Bayly Pike, a company secretary, and wife Ellen, of Christchurch, Hampshire.

Pike was particularly active as an artist in the 1880s and 1890s, exhibiting at the major London galleries and the Royal Academy. He painted scenes of the New Forest and the countryside around Bournemouth and Christchurch, as well as along the banks of the Rivers Avon and Stour and around his various London homes.

Pike was particularly known for those pictures in which he captured the atmosphere of the seasons. These included his well-known *Winter Landscape* which has featured on many Christmas Cards and is still used today.

Pike never seemed to settle for long in one place. However, during the 1870s and early 1880s he, his wife Katie and their children (three of whom were born in Herne Hill) lived at 35 Herne Hill Road, in a house they shared with a dentist. The family later moved to Taplow, Polesdown, then Christchurch, before returning to live in Belgravia and Chelsea. Sidney Pike died 4 December 1923, at the St Leonards-on-Sea home of his sister Emily.

## Thomas Pell Platt (1799-1852)
## Casino House, 3 Herne Hill
## Biblical Translator

After completing his education at Trinity College, Cambridge, Thomas Pell Platt became librarian to the British and Foreign Bible Society where he published a number of important works. The first was a catalogue of Ethiopic biblical manuscripts held in London and Paris, followed by a collation of the Ethiopic versions of the New Testament, which he edited. In 1829 he published an edition of The Gospels in Syriac, and in 1844, an Amharic version of the Bible. Platt was also a member of the Royal Asiatic Society and served for many years on its oriental translation committee.

In 1829, on the death of his father, Platt inherited Childs Hill House, Hampstead, near Golders Green and lived there with his wife, Ann and their three children, Anne, Francis and Mary. Platt died 31 October 1852 aged 53 at Casino House, Herne Hill, home of his brother-in-law, William Stone. Platt's sister Mary, who died in 1837, was Stone's first wife. Martha Platt, another sister, was a regular visitor or possibly house-keeper for a time.

## Patricia Plunkett (1926-74)
## 48 Half Moon Lane
## Actress

Patricia Ruth Plunkett was born at the Manor Nursing Home, Leigham Avenue, Streatham 17 December 1926. Her father, Gunning Francis Plunkett, worked at the Australian High Commission and her mother, Alice, was a light opera singer. The Plunketts moved to 48 Half Moon Lane in 1934.

Patricia attended St Martin-in-the-Fields High School, Tulse Hill. After a time spent as an evacuee, in 1944 on the death of her father she returned to 48 Half Moon Lane and started at the Royal Academy of Dramatic Art. Whilst appearing as Juliet, in a RADA production of *Romeo and Juliet*, she was spotted by a theatrical agent. As a result she was given a part in her first West End play *Stage Door* (1946). But it was her appearance later the same year in the title role of *Pick-Up Girl* at the Prince of Wales Theatre that made her a star.

Patricia joined the famous Rank Charm School, run by the Rank film company to groom potential future stars. Her first film role and one for which she gained much praise, was in the 1947 melodrama *It Always Rains on Sunday*. Throughout the 1950s she appeared in a number of West End productions, as well as another ten films. Of her films, the most notable were *Mandy* (1952) and *Dunkirk* (1958). Her last film was the 1960 crime melodrama *Escort for Hire*.

Patricia also appeared in television drama series such as *OSS* (1957) and *The Man From Interpol* (1961).

Patricia lived with her family at 48 Half Moon Lane until the early 1950s. On 27 October 1951 she married John Turner, an actor and television presenter.

After her acting career had ended, she moved to Lancing in Sussex, and set up in business as an antiques dealer. Patricia died on 15 October 1974, at St Stephen's Hospital, Chelsea, after accidentally choking on a piece of meat in a restaurant.

## Christopher Pond (1826-81)
## The Cedars, 62 Herne Hill
## Restaurateur

Born in Camberwell, Christopher Pond was the son of John Pond, a Customs official. He first comes to notice in the 1850s in Melbourne, Australia, probably lured there by the gold rush of that time.

With his partner, another expatriate Felix William Speirs (c1832-1911), Pond went into the catering business. They provided the expanding city of Melbourne with a chain of respectable licensed cafés. They bought the Café de Paris in Melbourne and also became co-proprietors of the café attached to Melbourne's Theatre Royal. Their success was sealed when they acquired the contract to supply refreshments to the Melbourne - Ballarat Railway.

In 1862 Pond travelled to England to promote his idea of cricket matches between representative England and Australia sides. An England team was recruited that included H H Stephenson and six other Surrey cricketers. Sailing on Brunel's SS Great Britain, the team arrived in Melbourne Christmas Eve 1862. A great success, the tour was cricket's first commercial sponsorship venture. Pond reputedly made a profit of £10,000, mainly from side bets.

***Pond (left) and Speirs***

The following year Speirs and Pond decided to sell their Australian enterprises and returned to England with the idea of improving the poor state of railway catering. Operating from 38 New Bridge Street, Blackfriars, they obtained the franchise on the new Metropolitan Railway; and later, on the London, Chatham and Dover Railway, to manage train dining cars and station refreshment rooms.

Their biggest venture was to build the new Criterion Theatre at 218-223 Piccadilly, in 1874. This was designed by architect Thomas Verity (1837-91) and cost £80,000. In addition to the theatre and restaurant, there were banqueting rooms on the upper floors.

The company eventually owned 12 hotels, including the Grand Hotel at Brighton. It was acquired by Chicken Inns in 1957 and by Grand Metropolitan Hotels in 1969.

About 1870, Pond moved to 62 Herne Hill, once occupied by Christopher Graham. He named it The Cedars and lived there until the end of his life. He died 30 July 1881 at his second home, Updown House, Margate, and left £221,775 in his will. He is buried at Norwood Cemetery, where his mausoleum is listed Grade II.

## Samuel Prout (1783-1852)
## 5 de Crespigny Terrace
## Artist

Samuel Prout was born in Plymouth 17 September 1783, the fourth of 14 children of Samuel Prout Sr, naval outfitter. Whilst a child he suffered an attack of sunstroke that was said to be the cause of the disabling headaches he suffered throughout his life. Having been encouraged to study painting when at Plymouth Grammar School, he tried, at first rather unsuccessfully, to make a living as an illustrator. However, he worked hard to improve his style; by 1803 he had exhibited at the Royal Academy and his career as a watercolourist had begun to prosper.

Around 1810 Prout moved to London and married Elizabeth Gillespie (1788-1863); they had four children. They lived at 4 Brixton Place, Stockwell 1810-35, briefly in Clapham and at Hastings for nine years. In 1845 they moved to 5 de Crespigny Terrace (see Robert Hunter), where they lived until Prout's death.

Prout specialised in watercolour paintings of buildings. It was during a visit to France that he found his niche painting gothic buildings "with great precision in a natural but picturesque style with good use of natural light and shade". He went on to publish books of his sketches and paintings as well as a number of drawing manuals. By 1830, Prout was regarded as one of the top half-dozen watercolour painters exhibiting in London, and his books made him widely known. He was later

championed by John Ruskin, who described Prout in his book *Modern Painters* as a "substantial and sunny colourist" and said "there is no stone drawing, no vitality of architecture like Prout's".

Constant ill health did not stop Prout travelling widely in Europe. However, after a trip to Normandy in 1846 he became so ill that he had to give up travelling; but continued to work, producing around 60 drawings a year, mainly for published lithographs. Prout died of a stroke in his painting room 10 February 1852. He was buried in Norwood Cemetery. After his death, Prout's widow and family moved to Ilfracombe, Devon.

### Sax Rohmer (1883-1959)
### 51 Herne Hill
### Author

Arthur Henry Ward was born 15 February 1883 at 28 Rann Street, Ladywood, Birmingham. He was the only child of Irish immigrants, William Ward and Margaret Mary Furey, who married in 1879. The family moved to South London when Arthur was two or three. Margaret, a voracious reader and alcoholic, claimed descent from 17th century general, Patrick Sarsfield. When she died of tuberculosis in 1901, Arthur took Sarsfield as a middle name.

Living with his father in Stockwell Road, working as a clerk, then a reporter, he sent stories and sketches to popular magazines. *The Mysterious Mummy*, which began the genre of Egyptian mummy horror stories, and *The Leopard-Couch* were accepted in 1903. He sold further tales, and joined a group of Balham bohemians in schemes to be theatrical agents, chemists, etc.

In 1905 he met Rose Elizabeth Knox, daughter of comedian and theatre lessee George Thomas Knox and dancer Julia Phillips. Elizabeth's seven siblings included Teddy Knox, later of the Crazy Gang. They courted, continually interrupted by Elizabeth's stage tours with her brother Bill, and married secretly on 14 January 1909. William and Arthur had moved to 24 Wyke Gardens, north Brixton; however, when the latter's first book, *Pause!*, was published in 1910, the young couple admitted their secret. William used his savings for a deposit on a house, 6 Danecroft Gardens, subsequently renumbered 51 Herne Hill. The trio moved in early 1911.

Buying their furniture on instalment and frequently pawning the silver, Arthur needed to make money. Having taken the pen-name Sax Rohmer, from the Saxon for 'blade' plus 'roamer' respelled, he produced magazine stories, songs and a ghosted 'Autobiography' of comedian Little Tich.

A commission for an article on a mysterious 'Mr King' of the Limehouse Chinatown underworld inspired Sax. His frequent visits there resulted in the creation of Fu-Manchu, criminal mastermind. Originally published as ten episodes in *The Story-Teller* from October 1912, *The Mystery of Dr. Fu-Manchu* appeared in book form in 1913.

At Herne Hill Sax wrote 15 novels, including the first three (of 13) Fu-Manchu books (the hyphen was later dropped). He also wrote a non-fiction work, *The Romance of Sorcery*, much admired by Harry Houdini, who became a firm friend. With his first success, the Rohmers took a belated honeymoon to Egypt; his travels and studies of eastern culture and the occult informed his writing. His stories began to appear in the US; and *The Yellow Claw* was filmed in Cricklewood in 1921.

That year, his growing celebrity induced Sax to move the family to Bruton Street, in fashionable Mayfair. Elizabeth regretfully resigned herself to parting with their Herne Hill home. In the years that followed, Sax's life and career had highs and lows; they moved several times, their final home being in Surrey. At one impecunious stage, his father William Ward returned to South London, taking digs in Denmark Hill.

An affair with a woman named Eve threatened the Rohmer marriage for a time. Sax also fell prey to unscrupulous agents, defrauding him of his profits. Faced with changing tastes and the demise of fiction magazines, he found new success with detective stories and a series featuring glamorous femme fatale Sumuru.

Sax Rohmer was renowned for his thrilling tales with exotic atmosphere. In all, he published 41 novels, eleven short story collections, two non-fiction books, several dozen articles, radio and television adaptations. There have been 14 Fu Manchu films, including three serials, with notable portrayals by Boris Karloff and Christopher Lee.

On 1 June 1959, Sax Rohmer died of Asian flu. In 1985 the GLC placed a Blue Plaque on 51 Herne Hill.

## Alfred Arthur Rouse (1894-1931)
## 242 Milkwood Road
## Murderer

Alfred Arthur Rouse was born 6 April 1894, the son of shopkeepers of 242 Milkwood Road. When he was six his parents separated and he was sent to live with an aunt.

Having finished school, Alfred spent five years working for a West End soft furnishers. He enlisted as a private in the army on 8 August 1914. On 29 November 1914 he married Lily May Watkins; the following May he was posted to France. After ten days, on 25 May, he was severely wounded in his head, thigh and leg by a shell burst. After treatment and convalescence he returned to England, and in 1916 was discharged from the army as no longer fit for active service. Alfred's personality appeared to have changed as a result of his head wound and it was said that he was never the same again.

Following his army discharge, Alfred had a variety of jobs before becoming a commercial traveller for a firm of braces and garter manufacturers. He took full advantage of the opportunity this gave him for seduction. It is said he had affairs with over 80 women. They fell ready victim to his handsome

appearance, plausible tongue and ingratiating manners. He had no children with his wife but at least six by other women, one of whom lived with Alfred and Lily in a house they had bought in Finchley.

By 1930, the costs of keeping his Finchley home, paying child maintenance orders as well as the household expenses from at least one bigamous marriage meant that, on a weekly income of eight pounds, Alfred's debts were out of control. He therefore conceived a plan to fake his own death and start life again with all his problems behind him.

On 6 November 1930, a burning car with a body inside was discovered on a road just east of Northampton. The car was identified as belonging to Alfred, but the body was burnt beyond recognition. Unluckily for him, two men had spotted Alfred near the car and he was later seen and recognised from pictures in the newspapers. Alfred was arrested. He told the police that he had picked up a hitchhiker and later, when he had got out of the car to answer a call of nature, it had caught fire causing him to panic and run away.

Alfred was charged with the murder of an unknown man and brought to trial on 26 January 1931 at Northampton Assizes. The trial took six days. Technical evidence showed that the car's carburettor had been tampered with before the fire had started; and a mallet belonging to Alfred - possibly the murder weapon - was found nearby. The jury took just 75 minutes to return a guilty verdict. His appeal having failed, Alfred was hanged at Bedford prison on 10 March 1931. The identity of the victim remains unknown.

Number 242 Milkwood Road was located opposite Lowden Road. In the 1960s, along with other houses in that stretch of Milkwood Road, it was demolished to make way for the present commercial estate.

## Arthur Rule (c1826-1915)
## 141 Railton Road
## Yeoman of the Guard

Chelmsford-born Arthur Rule was sent to the Crimea as a private in the 20$^{th}$ Foot (Lancashire Fusiliers), returning a sergeant-major, with the Imperial Order of the Legion of Honour. He was an eye-witness to the charge of the Light Brigade at Balaclava. Later he served as a staff-sergeant-major in the Post Office Rifle Volunteers, and after sixteen years took a commission, retiring with the honorary rank of major. He joined the Queen's Body Guard of the Yeoman of the Guard, serving for 49 years and reaching the rank of Messenger Sergeant Major.

From the 1870s, Rule lived at 141 Railton Road, next to the Methodist Church. He died there 5 June 1915, and is buried in Norwood Cemetery. His wife Eliza predeceased him in 1909.

## John Ruskin (1819-1900)
## 28 Herne Hill, 163 Denmark Hill and 30 Herne Hill
## Writer, Artist, Art and Social Critic

John Ruskin was one of the most influential intellectual and cultural figures of his age. In his later years some of his ideas were regarded as eccentric, and his views on art became increasingly unfashionable during the 20th century. However, the value of his writings about the environment, building conservation, the paintings of J M W Turner, art education, and the human cost of industrialisation has now become more recognised. The quality of his own drawings and watercolours is also better appreciated, as is his contribution to the success of 19th century British painting, architecture, and decorative art. Even though his style can sometimes appear difficult to the modern reader, Ruskin has also been rediscovered as one of the great writers of English prose.

Ruskin was born at 54 Hunter Street, London, 8 February 1819, the only child of John James Ruskin and Margaret Cox, daughter of a Croydon publican. John James Ruskin was chief partner in the firm of Ruskin, Telford, and Domecq, sherry and wine importers and distributors. The business prospered such that, in 1823, John James could afford to rent a house on Herne Hill. In 1842 the Ruskins moved to a much larger property, 163 Denmark Hill (demolished in 1947 to make way for the present blocks of flats).

Ruskin had a rather austere and lonely upbringing, although his suggestion that no toys were allowed may have been an exaggeration. Taught by his mother and by private tutors, he had little contact with other children; but at 14 he was sent as a day-boy to a small school (only five boys) in Grove Lane. An early interest in art and architecture was stimulated by family visits to France, Switzerland and Italy, as well as by his father's growing art collection. This included many watercolours by Turner, whom Ruskin was later to champion.

The intense relationship between father, mother and son had a major influence on Ruskin throughout his life. Realising their son's potential, his parents encouraged him to draw and write when still very young (his first poems were published when he was only ten). Every morning, from the age of three, his mother made him read from the Bible and learns passages by heart, perhaps reflecting her ambitions for him to enter the Ministry.

In January 1837 Ruskin entered Christ Church, Oxford, as a Gentleman Commoner, to read Classical Greats. His mother accompanied him, taking rooms in the town. Unlike many of his aristocratic companions, he took his studies seriously and completed his degree. In 1839 his efforts won him the Newdigate Prize for poetry.

In April 1840 he coughed blood; tuberculosis was suspected and he had to withdraw from the university, returning to Herne Hill. On medical advice, his parents took him on a European tour, lasting nine months and reaching Naples. It was at this time that Ruskin began work on what was to become his five-volume book *Modern Painters*: the first volume was published in 1843, but the whole project took another 17 years to complete. Thus began a successful literary and intellectual career. Fortunately, his father's patronage relieved him of the need to earn a living.

Following a period of depression in 1847, Ruskin's focus turned towards architecture, an interest stimulated during a visit to Italy two years previously, where he had discovered the Italian Romanesque. However, Venetian Gothic was always his favoured style, and his three-volume book *The Stones of Venice* (1851-53) was hugely influential on the Gothic Revival in Britain and America.

In April 1848 Ruskin married Euphemia 'Effie' Gray (1828-97), whom he had first met when she was twelve years old. After a spell living in Mayfair, in 1852 the couple moved to a house at 30 Herne Hill, next door to his previous home. However, two years later Effie left him and in July 1854 the marriage was annulled on the grounds of non-consummation. Effie later married the painter and friend of her husband, John Everett Millais. Although this ended Ruskin's friendship with the artist, he still continued publicly to recognise his talent and to support the Pre-Raphaelites.

As well as arguing the case for preserving ancient buildings, in *The Seven Lamps of Architecture* (1849), Ruskin had also developed an interest in social questions. Attempts to promote the anti-capitalist views expressed in *Unto This Last* (1862) were unsuccessful and derided in the establishment press. However, they did help to develop a wider debate on the business ethics of the time. Ruskin put his principles into practice by giving regular drawing classes at the London Working Men's College. He later established the Guild of St George, with a museum, library and teaching collection in Sheffield, and supported a collective farming experiment at nearby Totley.

Ruskin continued to travel widely, but the death of his father in March 1864 forced a return to Herne Hill. He stayed in the Denmark Hill house with his mother, helped by a cousin, Joan Agnew, who became her companion. His father's legacy left Ruskin comparatively wealthy, and he began to dispense his money on a series of charitable and philanthropic schemes. Despite signs of mental illness, Ruskin's reputation grew. By the end of the 1860s, he had become a prominent commentator on art and social issues, with a large following.

His status was given formal recognition on his election as Oxford University's first Slade Professor of Fine Art in August 1869.

In the summer of 1871, Ruskin purchased Brantwood, a property on Coniston Water in the Lake District, the view from which he declared "the best in England". When his mother died later that year, he sold the house at 163 Denmark Hill, and from 1872 made his home at Brantwood. He also continued to spend time at 28 Herne Hill, which had been leased to Joan Agnew and her husband Arthur Severn: there Ruskin occupied his former nursery.

Although still working and travelling, Ruskin's health continued to decline, and in February 1878 he suffered a complete mental breakdown. A few months later he was beginning to recover, but ill health remained the reason for not attending the hearing in November of the libel suit brought against him by the painter James McNeill Whistler. In describing Whistler's picture *Nocturne in Black and Gold: The Falling Rocket*, Ruskin accused him of "flinging a pot of paint in the public's face," and called him a "coxcomb." Whistler won the suit but was awarded damages of only one farthing, becoming bankrupt from having to meet his own legal costs. Ruskin's expenses were paid by his friends.

Ruskin's output continued to decline and in 1881 and 1882 he suffered further, often violent, bouts of depression: the latter occurred whilst staying in Herne Hill. Joan Severn looked after him, and by January 1883 he was well enough to return to Oxford to be re-elected Slade Professor. He resigned the post two years later following a number of disagreements with the University. Despite further bouts of mental instability, Ruskin was able to work on his autobiography *Praeterita*, published in parts between 1885 and 1889. In that year he suffered another devastating breakdown, ending any hope of further work.

The following years were spent at Brantwood, where he was cared for by the Severns. Ruskin gradually retreated into silence. On 18 January 1900, now confined to his bed, he caught influenza and died peacefully two days later. Burial in Westminster Abbey was offered; but in accordance with his wishes, he was interred in Coniston churchyard. A memorial exhibition in the village developed into the present Ruskin Museum.

Although the contents of Brantwood were eventually dispersed after the deaths of the Severns, the house was rescued through the efforts of John Howard Whitehouse, who was able to recover much and open the house to the public in 1934. Whitehouse's uniquely comprehensive collection of Ruskin materials (manuscripts, books and drawings) is now held in the Ruskin Library at Lancaster University. It is in the care of the Ruskin Foundation, which also oversees Brantwood. More than a century after his death, Ruskin's reputation stands as high as ever.

**John James Ruskin (1785-1864)**
**28 Herne Hill**
**and 163 Denmark Hill**
**Wine Importer**

Born in Edinburgh 10 May 1785, John James Ruskin (JJR) was sent to London c1801, at the age of 16, to start in business. He had many jobs, including several years in the wine and sherry trade as manager at Gordon, Murphy & Co., later to become Sandeman's. In 1814 JJR left to form his own company, Ruskin, Telford & Domecq, importers of Spanish wines, of 7 Billiter Street in the City of London. The new firm included a sleeping partner, Henry Telford, who provided the capital, and a wine producer in Spain, Pedro Domecq (d 1839), who rarely came to England. JJR ran the business alone, employing two clerks. He was greatly helped by the boom in the wine trade after the Napoleonic wars.

Earlier, in c1808, JJR's father John Thomas Ruskin (1761-1817), a grocer with extravagant tastes, had become bankrupt and left Edinburgh, moving to Perth. This resulted in his niece, Margaret Cox (1781-1871), coming from Croydon to stay as housekeeper and companion to his wife, Catherine. JJR and Margaret were soon attracted to each other and engaged to be married. John Thomas Ruskin objected to the engagement, perhaps thinking his son could find a more suitable wife. However, in 1817 John Thomas Ruskin committed suicide, leaving crippling debts of nearly £4,000 which took JJR many years to clear.

On 2 February 1818, JJR married Margaret at Perth, after a nine year engagement. They lived at 54 Hunter Street, Brunswick Square in London, a Georgian terraced house (now gone). In 1819 their only child, John Ruskin, was born there. Their stay at Hunter Street lasted only four years, for in 1823 they moved to 28 Herne Hill "a three-storied semi-detached house (with garrets and basement)". The house, on the site now occupied by 26/28 Herne Hill, next to Dorchester Court, was demolished in 1923.

JJR often borrowed a 'travelling-chariot' belonging to his partner Telford, and the family went all over the country. This included trips to the Lake District and Scotland, a certain amount of business being combined with pleasure. JJR amassed a considerable art collection, mainly watercolours, including examples by Turner, Fielding, Prout, Cox and Roberts. He shared his son's liking for Turner's work and, between 1839-45, acquired 21 watercolours and the major oil painting, *The Slave Ship*.

In 1842, JJR's prosperity enabled him to move to 163 Denmark Hill, a large detached three-storied house standing in seven acres ( three hectares) of land. He lived there for the rest of his life. Here JJR could display his paintings, fill his cellar with wine and entertain his and his son's many literary, artistic and influential friends and acquaintances. The house was demolished in 1947; the site is now Blanchdowne, between Cross Court and Shaftesbury Court.

JJR died 3 March 1864. After his death, his wine and sherry company became Peter Domecq & Co., moving to Great Tower Street in the 1880s and ceasing business c1918. In his will, JJR left £120,000 plus property worth £3,000 to his son John. He is buried in the churchyard at Shirley near Croydon. John Ruskin's epitaph on the tombstone describes his father as "an entirely honest merchant."

### Kathleen Saintsbury (c1898-c1987)
### 57 Rutland Court, Flat 1 Abbey Mansions, Flat 1A Herne Hill Mansions
### Actress

Kathleen Saintsbury was born in 1898 or 1899 in Camden Town. Her father, H A (Harry Arthur) Saintsbury (d 1939), was an actor, particularly well known for his portrayals of Sherlock Holmes. Kathleen followed her father into the theatre, and when still a young girl joined Bransby Williams' company performing in this country and on tours to North America. She played leading roles in many of his productions, including his Dickens adaptations as well as Jim the cabin boy in his production of *Treasure Island*. Bransby Williams was a friend of H A Saintsbury and had promised that he would take good care of her. Kathleen

stayed with Bransby Williams' company for over 20 years and spoke of the deep affection and gratitude she felt towards her friend and mentor.

In 1922 Kathleen had married actor Robert (Hubert) Purser but continued her own acting career, appearing in a number of West End productions. However, in the 1930s Bransby Williams fell seriously ill and Kathleen gave up acting, willingly sacrificing her career to nurse him and to act as his secretary and housekeeper. She stayed with him until his death in 1961.

Kathleen and Bransby moved into the newly built 57 Rutland Court, Denmark Hill in 1938. During the war they moved to Flat 1, Abbey Mansions, which is a block of four purpose-built flats dating from around 1900. It is located behind 381 Milkwood Road and can be reached by a short path between the garage and No. 381. The block has been derelict since the early 1990s.

After Bransby Williams' death, Kathleen stayed in Abbey Mansions for a further 17 years before moving to the nearby Herne Hill Mansions, where she lived at Flat 1A until 1986. She also returned in a small way to acting, playing minor television roles, including two episodes of *Dixon of Dock Green* as well as a small part in the 1968 British film *Separation*. She also played Private Godfrey's sister 'Cissy' in a 1975 episode of *Dad's Army*.

## Samuel Sanders (c1742-1815)
## 168 Denmark Hill
## Landowner

Samuel Sanders was a wealthy timber merchant with premises at Pedlar's Acre, Lambeth, next to Westminster Bridge where County Hall now stands. In 1783 he bought 124 acres (52 hectares) of land in the Manor of Lambeth including some of the area we now know as Denmark Hill. From the 1790s Sanders built a number of elegant detached mansions fronting the road at Denmark Hill, letting them out on long leases. He lived at one of the larger houses, 168 Denmark Hill, later occupied by Charles Druce. Sanders started a trend, and by the middle of the 19th century a continuous line of fashionable mansions had been built along the Lambeth side of the road. They stretched from the present King's College Hospital to Herne Hill Station. Today, the only remaining houses on the west side dating from that period are 10/12 Herne Hill and 164 Denmark Hill.

***Sanders' Denmark Hill House***

On 10 July 1815 Sanders died at Denmark Hill; he is buried at St Giles Church, Camberwell. His family moved from Denmark Hill, the ownership of the freehold properties passing first to his eldest son, Samuel Sanders (d 1859), who lived at a house called Fernhill on the Isle of Wight; then to his grandson, Arthur Sanders (1826-86) and great-grandson, Robert Arthur Sanders (1867-1940).

Robert Arthur Sanders served as an MP (1910-29), including a period as a junior minister (1918-24). He was created a baronet in 1920 and Lord Bayford in 1929. About 1905 he sold some of his Denmark Hill land to the LCC to establish Ruskin Park.

## Dr Marcus Scott (1900-78)
## 19 Dorchester Court
## Surgeon-in-Chief
## St John Ambulance

Marcus Scott was born 3 August 1900. He studied medicine at the Welsh National School of Medicine, Cardiff, and completed his clinical training at University College Hospital, qualifying as MRCS and LRCP in 1927. After some locum work he took an appointment at Guy's Hospital, where he stayed for over 40 years.

Dr Scott had a particular interest in industrial medicine and was medical advisor to a number of manufacturing companies as well as a Factory Doctor for the London Borough of Southwark. He was adviser on first aid to the Post Office Chief Medical Officer, a Police

Surgeon (1946-67) and a Senior Lecturer at the Metropolitan Police Training School (1938-68). He also contributed to many publications on first aid.

His great interest in first aid led him, in 1931, to join the St John Ambulance Brigade as Divisional Surgeon to the Newington St Andrews Division. He transferred in 1933 to 58/5 Western District Post Office and St Marylebone Division. During the war Dr Scott was Medical Officer in charge of the Southwark Mobile Hospital First Aid Unit – covering one of the most heavily blitzed areas in the country. He was out on duty every night, his skill and perseverance saving many lives and relieving much suffering. Dr Scott became St John Ambulance District Surgeon for London in 1947. In 1951 he was appointed Deputy Surgeon-in-Chief and Surgeon-in-Chief in 1966 - a post he held until his retirement in 1970.

For his work in Civil Defence and for St John Ambulance he was awarded the CBE in 1971.

Dr Scott lived with his wife Eva at 19 Dorchester Court from 1951 until his death on 21 June 1978.

## Arthur Severn (1842-1931)
## 28 Herne Hill
## Artist

Joseph Arthur Palliser Severn's father was Joseph Severn (1793-1879), a painter who joined the circle of the poet John Keats in 1816. He had attended Keats at his death in 1821, and was the British Consul in Rome from 1860 to 1872.

One of six children, Arthur and his twin sister Eleanor were born in London 14 August 1842. He was educated at Westminster School, and then studied art with his father in Rome from 1862-64, continuing his studies in Paris in 1868. On returning to London he exhibited seven drawings

***Joan Agnew***

at the Dudley Gallery. Having sold all of them, he decided to take up art as a profession, exhibiting at the Royal Academy, the Royal Institute and in Paris.

In 1871 he married Joan Agnew, the second cousin and ward of John Ruskin, and was given Ruskin's old family home, 28 Herne Hill, as a wedding present. The Severns kept the former nursery for Ruskin's use whenever he visited London, as by that time he had moved to Brantwood, at Coniston in the Lake District.

During the 1890s Arthur and Joan moved to Brantwood to care for John Ruskin until he died in 1900; their five children also spent much time there. They inherited Brantwood and a large sum of money. However, they did not meet all Ruskin's wishes regarding the property. He had wanted the Severns to "accord 30 consecutive days in every year to strangers to see the house and pictures as I have done in my lifetime." Instead, they advertised that the house was not open to the public, establishing a memorial exhibition in the village, now the Ruskin Museum. Arthur's personal recollections of Ruskin have been published as *The Professor*.

In 1907 the Severns gave up the Herne Hill lease, and made their London home at 9 Warwick Square, Pimlico. The house at 28 Herne Hill remained empty until it was demolished in 1923. After Joan's death in 1924, Arthur moved back to London. A series of sales, starting at Sotheby's in 1930, dispersed the contents of Brantwood, including paintings, furniture, books and manuscripts. John Howard Whitehouse, a former Secretary of the Ruskin Society of Birmingham and a keen disciple of Ruskin, was able to make substantial purchases. Many of these he returned to the house, which he also bought in 1932.

Arthur Severn died 23 February 1931 at his London home, leaving £12,480 in his will.

## Richard Shawe (c1755-1816)
## Casino House, 3 Herne Hill
## Solicitor

Shawe (or Shaw) was a respected London solicitor, becoming head of the firm of Shawe, LeBlanc and Shawe of Bridge Street, Blackfriars. He built Casino (or Casina) House in 1796, a country house retreat within easy reach of the City. The architect John Nash (1752-1835), who was collaborating with Repton at that time, is thought to have designed the house, which was built on land leased from Dulwich College Estate. It had a handsome Doric portico, and was one of the first mansions on Herne

***Shawe's tomb in Dulwich Burial Ground***

Hill/Denmark Hill (then called Dulwich Hill). The landscape designer Humphrey Repton (1752-1818) laid out the 15 acre (six hectare) garden. The house was demolished in 1906; the site is now commemorated by the Sunray/Casino Estate around Casino Avenue, built 1920-22 by the Metropolitan Borough of Camberwell. Sunray Gardens is a small park created in 1922 from the water gardens designed by Repton.

As solicitor, Shawe was responsible for the defence for Warren Hastings (1732-1818) at his spectacular trial at Westminster Hall. The trial lasted for seven years (1788-95). Hastings, who is remembered today for having laid the foundations of British India, served as Governor-General of Bengal (1774-85); but on his return to England, he was accused of partiality and high-handedness. Parliament impeached Hastings on charges of mismanagement of funds; he was eventually acquitted. After this lengthy court case Shawe spent £40,000 on building Casino House. By coincidence or not, this was thought to be the same sum that Hastings had brought back with him from India.

Shawe died 11 August 1816 at another of his properties, Hamells Park, Hertfordshire. He is buried in Dulwich Burial Ground where his impressive tomb can be seen from Court Lane. He married three times and had a daughter and three sons. He was survived by his third wife, Anne Bogle French, whom he had married at St Giles Church, Camberwell in 1806.

Later occupants of Casino House included William Stone from 1839-57, William Henry Stone from 1857-c1880 and William Sutton Gover from c1880-94.

## Lord Shelburne (1816-66)<br>32 Herne Hill<br>Member of Parliament

As the eldest son of the 3rd Marquess of Lansdowne (1780-1863), Henry Petty Fitzmaurice was entitled to the courtesy title of Lord Shelburne or Earl of Shelburne. Henry's grandfather, William Petty (1737-1805), also Lord Shelburne and later 1st Marquess of Lansdowne, had been Prime Minister (1782-83), and his father, the 3rd Marquess was in the Cabinet for many years, serving as Chancellor of the Exchequer (1806-07).

Born 5 January 1866, Henry was educated at Trinity College, Cambridge, and from 1837-56 was returned as the Whig MP for Calne in Wiltshire, near his father's country home of Bowood. He served as Lord of the Treasury (1847-48) and as Under Secretary for Foreign Affairs (1856-58).

***Shelbourne Coat-of-Arms***

Although living at his father's London home, Lansdowne House, 54 Berkeley Square, Lord Shelburne's name appears in the Lambeth Rate returns for 1839-40 as a resident of Herne Hill. (No rate returns exist for years 1835-38.) He probably lived at Herne Hill Cottage, 32 Herne Hill, the former home of Anna Storace (site now occupied by 5 Dorchester Drive), though he left before the 1841 census was taken. In 1840 he married Lady Georgiana Herbert, fifth daughter of the 11th Earl of Pembroke. Georgiana died in 1841; and in 1843 Shelburne married Emily Jane Mercer Elphinstone de Flahault (d 1895). He died 5 July 1866.

On Henry's death, his eldest son, Henry Charles Keith Petty Fitzmaurice (1845-1927), succeeded him as the 5th Marquess. The son had a distinguished career, serving as Governor-General of Canada (1883-88), Viceroy of India (1888-94 and Foreign Secretary (1900-05).

## Rt Rev. Bertram Fitzgerald Simpson (1883-1971)
## 62 Half Moon Lane
## Bishop of Southwark

Bertram Simpson was born 25 September 1883. He graduated from Durham University with a first class degree in theology and was appointed Deacon and later Priest at St Anne's church in Soho. In 1912 he married Ethyl Mary Penistan (d 1952). They had a son and a daughter. From 1913 to 1920 Bertram was Vicar of St Peter's in Harrow. For two of these years (1916-18) he was an army Chaplain. In 1918 he was awarded the Military Cross "for conspicuous gallantry and devotion to duty" for continuing with his work in the forward-most front line, despite having been injured by a shell burst.

After Harrow, Bertram moved to a church in Stepney, then in 1926 to St Peter's, Cranley Gardens, South Kensington. In 1932 he was appointed Suffragen Bishop of Kensington, then he became Bishop of Southwark in 1942, a position he held until his retirement in 1958. His many other appointments included Honorary Chaplain to the King, from 1919 to 1932.

Bertram was known as one of the greatest preachers of his generation, renowned for his fervent and impassioned sermons (given without notes) and for his remarkable command of language. He was also highly regarded for his kindly and sympathetic character and for his devotion to his diocese. On his retirement in 1959 Bertram moved to 62 Half Moon Lane, where he lived with his daughter Joan, until his death on 16 July 1971. The house, now demolished, occupied the currently empty plot on the corner of Half Moon Lane and Delawyk Crescent.

## Thomas Simpson (c1747-1835) and Sarah (c1761-1847) 52 Herne Hill Philanthropists

Thomas Simpson was a partner in North, Simpson and Graham, grocers and tea dealers, of New Bridge Street, Blackfriars, and a colleague of Christopher Graham. From the 1810s, he lived with his wife Sarah at 52 Herne Hill. The house was demolished in the late 1880s; 82 and 84 Herne Hill now occupy the site. Thomas and Sarah leased six acres of land from the Dulwich College Estates located immediately opposite their house, possibly to prevent any building there that would spoil their view. In 1843, Sarah (by then a widow) gave some of this leased land on which to build a church at Herne Hill, to be called St Paul's. The church was consecrated in December 1844. Mrs Simpson also gave money to buy the sacramental plate.

In 1834, Thomas and Sarah gave land for a school, which was established in West Place (now part of Railton Road) to provide Christian education for the

***St Paul's School c1844***

infant poor living in West Place, Herne Place and Regent Row (now Regent Road). The school became known as St Paul's School in 1844 and St Jude's School in 1869. It moved to new premises in the 1970s; the old building is now used by the Temple of Truth Pentecostal Church.

Simpson's Alley was a field path that marked the old parish boundary between Camberwell and Lambeth, running alongside the Simpson's land. John Ruskin often used this path on his walks to Dulwich and referred to it in his autobiography *Praeterita*. The road marking the path's route is now called Ruskin Walk.

Thomas Simpson died 1 May 1835 aged 88, "after a life of exemplary piety and benevolence". Sarah died 12 May 1847 aged 85. She is buried alongside her husband in a vault at St Matthew's Church, Brixton. The couple had no children.

## George Albert Smith (1864-1959) 2 Howletts Road Film Pioneer

George Smith was born 4 January 1864 in Cripplegate, east London. After his father's death, his mother moved the family to Brighton where she ran a boarding house. George started his

working life as a portrait photographer, diversifying later into presenting magic lantern shows. He also worked as a fortune teller, stage hypnotist, psychic and pleasure garden operator. Inspired by the work of the Lumière brothers, George acquired his first movie camera in 1897. Over the next twelve years he made over 40 films, mostly comedies and fairy tales. His wife Laura starred in many of these. In 1903 he made a film in Dulwich titled *52 Dancers Dressed as Playing Cards*. He also filmed regularly at the Crystal Palace.

George was one of the first film-makers to explore fictional and fantastic themes, often using quite sophisticated special effects, including some of the first 'glass shots'. He used double-exposure - using his own patented system - to achieve ghostly effects. In 1906, with his partner Charles Urban (1867-1942), he produced an early colour process called Kinemacolor. Kinemacolor films did well until the First World War, but litigation over the patent led to the system being abandoned. This effectively ended his life in the film business. In his later years, he spent much of his time pursuing his passion for astronomy.

George Smith spent most of his life in Hove. In 1866 he was living in Dulwich. He then moved to Kent before coming to 2 Howletts Road, where he lived from 1891 to 1895. George died in Brighton General Hospital on 17 May 1959. Hove Museum houses a permanent display of his work.

## Dr Julian E Spindel (1925-2001)
## 89 Dorchester Court
## Civil Engineer

Dr Julian Erwin Spindel was born 8 September l925 in Innsbruck, Austria. His father was Dr M Spindel, a Civil Engineer who as Head Government Surveyor of Works in Austria was renowned for his expertise in bridge building. Like his father, Julian also became an outstanding Civil Engineer, specialising in railway bridge design.

Dr Spindell came to England with his family some time before the war. He was educated at Dulwich College, then studied engineering at Imperial College. He began his career in the Bridge Office of British Railways Southern Region. From there he moved to the Midland Region as the engineer in charge of all bridge design work. This included work connected with electrifying the line from London to Manchester and Liverpool. He then moved to the British Railways Board Headquarters where he was appointed Bridge Development Engineer.

In 1961 Dr Spindell became a member of the British Standards Institution (BSI) committee for bridge design codes. Until 1978 he continued working on the BSI and European committees that covered the development of the Civil/Structural engineering codes and specifications. In 1992, the BSI awarded him its Distinguished Service Certificate "in appreciation of long and valued contributions to the development of British, European and international Standards". In 1996 he was awarded the MBE for "service to the Railway industry and to Bridge Engineering".

Dr Julian Spindell went to live at 89 Dorchester Court in 1952, staying there until his death in April 2001.

## William Stone (c1793-1857)
## Casino House, 3 Herne Hill
## Silk Merchant

Born at Piccadilly, William Stone was a silk merchant with a large interest in the firm of Pawson & Co, warehousemen of St Paul's Churchyard in the City of London. In 1828 he married Mary Platt at Christ Church, Blackfriars Road; they had two sons and two daughters. About 1832 they moved to 186 Denmark Hill. The house, demolished in the 1930s, was on the site of the present Acland Crescent. Mary died there in 1837; she is buried at St Matthew's Church, Brixton. In 1839, the family moved to Casino House, the large country house built in 1796 for the solicitor Richard Shawe.

In 1843, Stone gave £315 towards the £6,707 building costs of the planned St Paul's Church in Herne Hill. The size of his donation was second only to the contribution from the Church Commissioners. He became patron of Herne Hill parish, providing the stipend to the clergy. In 1852, Stone paid for the building of St John's Church in Angel Town, Brixton and also became patron there.

After Mary died, Stone remained a widower for many years. As well as his own children, at various times his house was home to many of his nephews and nieces. In 1853, he married Catherine Hayley. In his will, Stone expressed the wish to be buried next to his first wife at St Matthew's, Brixton. However, when he died in August 1857, the family decided to bury him at Norwood Cemetery, where he lies alone. He was survived by his second wife and by his youngest son, William Henry Stone, and two daughters.

## William Henry Stone (1834-96)
## Casino House, 3 Herne Hill
## Member of Parliament

Educated at Harrow and Trinity College, Cambridge, where he studied law, William Henry Stone was the second but only surviving son of William Stone of Casino House. On the death of his father in 1857, he inherited the House and about £300,000.

With his new-found wealth Stone bought Leigh Park, a large property at

Havant in Hampshire in 1861. There he commissioned a Cambridge friend, architect Richard William Drew (1834-1903), to design a new house for him. Stone became Lord of the Manor of Havant and Flood, Magistrate for Surrey (1861) and Magistrate for Hampshire (1863). In 1864 he married Mellicent Helps, second daughter of Sir Arthur Helps (1813-75), Dean to the Privy Council. In 1870, Stone contributed £500 towards the £1,500 building cost of the new Havant Town Hall and again commissioned Drew to prepare the plans. Stone was elected Liberal MP for Portsmouth in 1865, winning again in 1870 when a new parliamentary franchise operated.

Events at this time, however, forced Stone to make changes in his lifestyle. About 1868, his wealthy father-in-law, Sir Arthur Helps, had to relinquish his large estate at Bishops Waltham in Hampshire after an ambitious business venture ran into serious problems. In the election of 1874 Stone lost his Portsmouth seat and sold his estate at Leigh Park, moving to Norbury Park, Mickleham, Surrey. He contested Chatham in the 1875 election and Greenwich in 1880, but lost on both occasions.

William Henry Stone was patron of St Paul's Church, Herne Hill, a position his father had previously held. In 1865, as patron, he commissioned Drew to design the St Paul's vicarage, now Herne Hill School, 127 Herne Hill. In 1866, his wife Mellicent laid the foundation stone to St Saviour's Church in Herne Hill Road (this church was demolished in 1981). In 1881 Stone laid the foundation stone for St John's Church in Lowden Road. As an enthusiastic gardener, he allowed the annual Surrey Horticultural Show to be held in the grounds of Casino House. About 1880, after forty years in the Stone family, Casino House was sold. In the 1880s Stone moved to Lea Park, Witley, Surrey, where his wife died in 1891 aged 44. Soon after her death, Stone moved to Lower House, Thursley, Surrey where he died 7 November 1896 aged 61. He left just £8,997 in his will and was survived by his two children, Arthur and Mellicent.

## Anna Selina Storace (1765–1817)
## Herne Hill Cottage
## Singer

Anna Selina 'Nancy' Storace was the most important English soprano of the second half of the 18th century. She was born in London 27 October 1765 to her Italian father Stefano, a double-bass player at the Haymarket Opera House.

By the time she was eight, Anna was singing before royalty and performing throughout England. In 1778 the family moved to Italy and two years later she made her Italian debut in Florence. Here she was so popular that her fellow performer, the castrato Luigi Marchesi, demanded she be dismissed from the troupe. Anna went on to sing in Milan and Venice before moving to Vienna in 1783 to join the Italian Opera Company. Here she stayed for four years, enjoying great success with her fine voice, charming looks and spirited acting. One of her many roles was Susanna in the first performance of Mozart's *Marriage of Figaro*. She also performed works specially written for her by Mozart, Salieri and Cornetti.

In 1784, whilst in Vienna and after many love affairs, Anna married John Abraham Fischer (1744-1806), an English composer and violinist. The marriage was not a success, not least because of John's violent nature. His ill treatment of Nancy led to his expulsion from Austria. Nevertheless, in 1785 Anna gave birth to a daughter, who sadly did not survive.

Anna returned to London in 1787, again enjoying immense popularity and becoming a wealthy woman. Until his death in 1796 at the age of 33, she worked closely with her brother Stephen, a composer and conductor of popular comic operettas. By this time she was the highest paid singer at the Drury Lane Theatre, averaging ten guineas a performance.

In 1796, Anna met John Braham, a talented tenor eleven years her junior, who had sung in one of Stephen's operettas. Though unmarried, they lived together for the next 18 years. In 1797 they set off on a tour of Europe, singing for Napoleon and Josephine, before going on to Florence, Milan, Naples, Venice and Vienna. In Naples, they met Admiral Nelson and his mistress, Emma Hamilton, with whom Nancy formed a close, lifelong friendship.

The couple returned to London in 1801; the following May Anna gave birth to a son, William Spencer. She returned to the stage after William's birth, but five years later decided to retire.

Her final performance was on 30 May 1807, in her brother's operetta *No Song, No Supper*. In January 1809, the family moved into Herne Hill Cottage. This had been Anna's 'country home' since 1805. However, it was no cottage, having been refurbished by the architect Sir John Soane, with twelve rooms and four acres of ground.

John Braham, continuing his own career, was often absent from home. Their relationship finally broke down in 1814 when he left for another, much younger woman. There followed a serious decline in Anna's health, attributed so it was said to Braham's desertion.

Anna died of a stroke at 1.30pm on 24 August 1817 and was buried nine days later in the churchyard of St Mary's, Lambeth (now the Museum of Garden History). A memorial tablet to Anna, erected by her mother, can still be seen high up on the church's eastern wall.

Anna made her permanent home at Herne Hill Cottage from 1809 until her death. The cottage no longer exists, but was located where 5 Dorchester Drive now stands. It was entered by a drive between the present 32 Herne Hill and The Quadrangle. In the 1820s, John James Ruskin rented a house in the cottage's extensive grounds. This was demolished in 1923 and replaced by 26 and 28 Herne Hill.

## William Strudwick (c1834-1910)
## 44 Kestrel Avenue
## Pioneer Photographer

The photographs of William Strudwick have often been reproduced in books on Victorian London, but he has rarely received a proper credit. Most were merely signed as "photographer unknown" or "anon".

Strudwick was born at 61 Edgware Road, Paddington, the son of John Duffell Strudwick (1789-1840), a cabinet maker. The first evidence of his interest in photography was pre-1860, when he published a booklet entitled *Art of Photographic Etching*, which later ran to three editions. Photographic Etching is another term for 'wet-plate' photography. At the time of the 1861 census he was described as a photographic storekeeper, living with his mother at 2 Bolton Terrace. The site is now Ambergate Street, off Penton Place, Walworth.

In the 1860s Strudwick started taking photographs of London street scenes, especially recording buildings about to be demolished. His practice was to stop at a road junction, point his camera along each street and take a photograph. Invariably the people living there would come out to be included in the picture, making the photos all the more interesting. At the end of the 19th century he reminisced:

> "I gave a good deal of time to taking photographs in the streets of London .... The picturesque character of some parts of London (there are not so many now) had long been present to my mind. I found a good number of subjects in old Lambeth between Westminster and Vauxhall .... I made a large number of pictures...the negatives (12x10) of which I still have, but they have been little seen. In this work I was assisted very much by a large dark tent or house on wheels (a home-made one). It had a boarded floor and carried all the working plant, and was large enough for me to stand upright in, with ample elbow room .... This tent was drawn by a man, and on arriving at a given point, I could have a plate ready in ten minutes."

In 1867 his photographs taken prior to the construction of the Albert Embankment were sold to the Metropolitan Board of Works, the predecessor of the LCC; and in 1874 he was commissioned by them to photograph the pre-construction scenes of the Chelsea Embankment. In 1868-69 the Victoria and Albert Museum bought many of his prints, including those of the Lambeth riverside and views of Westminster and the City of London.

In 1868, at the parish church of St Mary, Newington, Strudwick married Julia Batchelor, daughter of George Batchelor, proprietor of a chemist shop at 187 Newington Butts (then 24 High Street, Newington). The couple moved to 68 Thurlow Park Road (then 4 Albany Villas).

***Strudwick: Half Moon Tavern c1880***

In the 1860s and 1870s Strudwick produced some very skilful drawings and paintings which he exhibited and sold at various London galleries. At this time he tended to describe himself as an artist or draughtsman rather than a photographer. He appears to have lost interest in outdoor photography by the 1880s; and the photographic studio he ran in Queen Victoria Street in 1882 was a financial failure. In 1891 he moved to a smaller house at 44 Kestrel Avenue, taking in boarders to make ends meet. These were hard times for Strudwick. In 1902 he moved again to 193 Portland Road, South Norwood. His wife died in 1906 and he moved finally to Frant Road, Thornton Heath. The combination of chronic bronchitis and a heart attack contributed to his death on 18 July 1910 at the Croydon Workhouse Infirmary, followed by a pauper's funeral.

After his death, Strudwick's collection of prints and negatives were deposited at Croydon Town Hall. In 1913, 79 negatives were acquired by Charles Woolley, who offered them, together with a collection of his own antiquarian prints and Lambeth pottery, to Lambeth Council for a proposed Lambeth museum. This never materialised and the collection is now stored at the Lambeth Archives in Minet Library.

## 'Big Ray' Sykes (c1921-2005)
## 54 Cambria Road
## Country and Western Entertainer

The 20 stone figure of 'Big Ray' Sykes was familiar around Herne Hill and as an entertainer in pubs from Kennington to Bermondsey, at venues such as the Skinners Arms, Camberwell, the Red Lion, Walworth and the Final Furlong in Bermondsey.

Big Ray was never seen without one of his many Stetson hats and genuine cowboy boots. Since c1956 he had lived in his "home on the range" with his wife Lilly in Cambria Road. Here he set up one room as an exhibition with cowboy hats, boots, buckles, buffalo horns, genuine western film posters, pictures of John Wayne and a country music disco.

When Big Ray reached 75 years of age, his wife appealed to Channel 4's *Big Breakfast Show*, 'Judge the Grudge' to help in her plea to stop him wearing his cowboy 'gear' when they were out together. Unfortunately for Lilly, the studio audience supported Big Ray telling him to carry on "walking tall".

Big Ray died on 7 May 2005 and was cremated at Honor Oak Cemetery, after being given a real cowboy funeral send-off.

## Joseph Thomas (1838-1901)
## 10 Woodquest Avenue
## Civil Engineer

Joseph Thomas was born 10 March 1838 in Roche, Cornwall. He was taught practical engineering while working for his father, a road, railway and harbour contractor. After a short spell at sea, he left his father's firm and

went to work on a variety of projects in Plymouth, the Hungarian State Railways, the Easton and Church Hope Railway in Portland, the new St Helier Harbour and, in 1872, the Corbière Lighthouse. The reputation he had gained led to his appointment, in 1878, as Assistant Engineer at the Royal Albert Dock, and six years later, Resident Engineer. In 1890 he left the docks and was given as a leaving present a theodolite and a 'handsomely illuminated address'. The company Chairman praised his great ability, energy and thorough knowledge of resources, in completing a work of great difficulty without interrupting the work of the docks. The Chairman quoted Wren's epitaph "*si monumentum quaeris circumspice*" - if you seek his monument, look around.

Elected to full membership of the Institution of Civil Engineers in 1889, then a significant honour, Joseph subsequently worked on a variety of projects at home and abroad. These included the Arizona Irrigation Canal, the International Docks at New York and a deep water landing pier at Milford Haven.

From about 1890, Joseph and his wife Mary Ann, whom he had married in 1859, moved to 10 Woodquest Avenue. They went there to live with their younger daughter, also Mary Ann, her husband William Tinkham (a solicitor's clerk) and grandson Billy. Joseph had bought land at Hannafore Point, West Looe, Cornwall, and visited there whenever he could to complete a number of projects for the town. His contribution to the welfare and expansion of Looe was immense. Work there included the tourist attractions of the Hannafore Estate, a railway link to the main Great Western line and the famous Banjo Pier. He died suddenly, on 14 August 1901, whilst staying with his wife's cousins in East Looe.

The Tinkhams and Mrs Thomas continued to live at 10 Woodquest Avenue until 1902. Nothing now remains of the house, as it was destroyed during an air raid on 19 March 1941, along with a number of other properties in Woodquest Avenue and Milkwood Road. The site is now occupied by post-war bungalows.

## Harold Thornton (1892-1958)
## 52 Holmdene Avenue
## Artist

Born in Lambeth, Francis Harold Thornton lived in South London all his days. In the summer of 1917 he married Florence Alice Grover (1887-1956) in Croydon; their son Leonard Harold was born early in 1920 at Lewisham. From 1920 to 1939 Harold was Art Master at Southwark Central School, while studying with Douglas Smart at Clapham School of Art from 1920-24, and William Palmer Robins at the Central School of Arts and Crafts from 1929-33. In 1934, the Thornton family moved to 52 Holmdene Avenue, where they lived for the rest of the artist's life.

After a spell at Hornsey School of Art from 1939-43 under John Moody, Harold Thornton exhibited at the Royal Academy between 1943 and 1958, showing 13 etchings and dry point works during that period. He also exhibited at The Society of Graphic Art, the Paris Salon and elsewhere overseas. An accomplished etcher, watercolour painter, engraver, pencil artist and poster designer, he specialised in landscapes and architectural views, including abbeys, cathedrals and castles as well as country cottages, harbours and seascapes. The Ministry of Works bought his pictures; two of his proof etchings are in the collection of HM the Queen, and the Southwark Art Collection holds his 1930 etching of Hillcrest Lodge, Herne Hill.

Harold died 13 April 1958.

NB Some sources confuse our Harold Thornton with another artist of the same name born in Burnley the same birth year, 1892. The latter had a completely separate career at Burnley Central School and Plymouth School of Art.

## Edward, Lord Thurlow (1731-1806) Knight's Hill House, Norwood Road Lord Chancellor

Edward, later to become the first Baron Thurlow, was born in Norfolk 9 December 1731, the eldest son of Thomas Thurlow, a Church of England clergyman. Whilst at school he quickly acquired, and never lost, a well-deserved reputation for recalcitrance and rudeness. When studying at Cambridge University, his ill-mannered and rebellious behaviour brought him into constant conflict with authority. In 1751 he withdrew from Cambridge without a degree, but went on to study law, being called to the bar in 1754.

Edward's early legal career was not very successful and at one point he considered leaving the profession. However, his ability quickly to master a brief, a courtroom manner one moment ferocious the next sardonic, his strong physical presence and his powerful oratory eventually brought him great success.

In 1765 Edward was elected MP for Tamworth, Staffordshire. He quickly rose to prominence and was made Solicitor General in 1770 and Attorney General the following year.

During the 1770s Edward developed a friendship with King George III. In 1778, feeling that the government needed strengthening to deal with the problems of the American War of Independence, the King appointed him Lord Chancellor. In the House of Lords, Edward maintained his aggressive and domineering approach to debate, much to the irritation of his fellow peers and

ministerial colleagues. At the same time, he also gained a reputation for being rather idle. However, despite the antagonism of colleagues, he remained in office for the next 14 years. He proved a very able Lord Chancellor, using his eloquence to carry through many sometimes unpopular measures.

Edward's bad-tempered outbursts and open criticisms of government policy eventually led to a breakdown of relations with Prime Minister William Pitt the Younger. This resulted in his being dismissed as Lord Chancellor in 1792. In compensation he was made Baron Thurlow of Thurlow, Suffolk.

Edward never married. However, in 1759 or 1760 he met Catherine (Kitty) Lynch, daughter of John Lynch, Dean of Canterbury. Kitty gave birth to Edward's son in 1760, but died in childbirth. Later, Edward formed a public relationship with Polly Humphries, the daughter of a coffee house proprietor. Their first child was still-born in 1771, but they went on to have three daughters.

Edward had been living at Knight's Hill Farm, near to what is now Elmcourt Road, Tulse Hill. In 1772 he bought the house along with an adjoining 100 acres, but decided to replace the building with something more suitable. The result was Knight's Hill House, completed around 1787/88. There was a dispute over the building costs. Edward had originally instructed the architect Henry Holland (1746-1806) not to exceed £6,000; but the eventual cost was three times that sum. The dispute with Holland was settled by arbitration. Edward now possessed a superb and extravagantly furnished mansion, surrounded by a magnificent park. The estate eventually covered over a thousand acres, incorporating most of the Lambeth land on the east side of Norwood Road, from Croxted Road to Robson Road. However, because of the dispute, he refused to move into his new home. It remained empty, a monument to Edward's stubbornness, until the estate was sold and the great mansion demolished in 1810.

Edward made his home in the nearby, but much more modest Thurlow House, a small house on his estate, towards Dulwich. He lived here with Polly for the rest of his life, though he made frequent visits to Brighton. It was during one of these visits, seeking relief from the gout, that he died on 12 September 1806. He was buried thirteen days later in the Temple Church, London.

## Frank Trier (1853-1923)
## 147 Denmark Hill
## Engineer & Founder of Ruskin Park

In 1904 an area of 24 acres (10 hectares) on the west side of Denmark Hill was to be sold for housing development. As a result of the persistent efforts of Frank Trier, the Ruskin Park Purchase Committee was formed with the purpose of establishing a new park on this site. Trier suggested the park should be named after John Ruskin, who had just died and had been a local resident. He thought that donations for the park might come from Ruskin's many admirers.

In 1783, the land had been bought by a wealthy timber merchant, Samuel Sanders, who then built a number of elegant detached mansions there. In 1906, thanks to Trier's committee, the land and eight houses (numbers 162-176 Denmark Hill) were purchased by the LCC from Robert Sanders (1867-

***Ruskin Park c1900***

1940), later Lord Bayford and great-grandson of Samuel Sanders.

Ruskin Park, which opened in 1907, was laid out by the LCC with financial help from Lambeth, Camberwell and Southwark Metropolitan Borough Councils, the Metropolitan Public Gardens Association and many private individuals. In 1909 a further twelve acres (five hectares), a former market garden between Finsen and Ferndene Roads, became available. Again thanks to Trier's committee, this area opened in 1910 as an extension to the park.

Frank Henry Trier was born to German parents in a house on the east side of Denmark Hill, possibly where the railway runs, at the corner with Champion Park. At the time of the 1861 census, the family had moved to 147 Denmark Hill, next to Champion Hill. Trier qualified as a civil engineer but practised as a mechanical engineer and was involved with his brothers in a business that manufactured lubricants. In 1892, he moved with his family to 6 The Terrace (later to become 59 Champion Hill - the site is now Langford Green). He moved again in 1906 to Uplands, 11 Champion Hill, a large house where Ruskin Park House flats now stand. He died 4 June 1923.

## Augustus Quackenbush Tucker (1839-1915)
## Onaway, 173 Half Moon Lane
## Patent Medicine Seller

Augustus Quackenbush Tucker was born 29 December 1839 on a farm in Washington County, New York State, USA, the son of Nathaniel and Jane Quackenbush Tucker. He took to farming, lumbering and teaching. In 1866, he married Julia McKellor (also from Washington County) and they moved to Ohio, settling at Gilhead Station where he became a partner in a saw-mill business, Smith and Tucker. They had four children.

Many years later, in 1901, they were living in London, England. Tucker was a seller of patent medicines with an address at 51 Holborn Viaduct. In the same year he built a house in Herne Hill. He named it Onaway after a character in the epic poem *The Song of Hiawatha* by Henry Wadsworth Longfellow (1807-82), set to music in 1900 by Samuel Coleridge-Taylor (1839-1912).

Located on the corner of Half Moon Lane and Ardbeg Road, the house displays an American Eagle, a Stars and Stripes motif and his initials "AQT" (all on the Ardbeg Road side).

On 9 June 1904, Tucker's wife Julia laid one of a number of memorial stones commemorating the building of Herne Hill Baptist Church in Half

Moon Lane. Julia died in Cairo, Egypt in 1905. Her body was brought back to England to be buried in Norwood Cemetery. Augustus died 25 December 1915 at Mercy Hospital, Chicago, Illinois. His body was transported to England to be buried with his wife. Onaway was converted into flats in 1926.

## Walter George Tucker (d 1958)
## 149 Half Moon Lane
## Patent Medicine Supplier

Walter George Tucker was the son of an American, Augustus Quackenbush Tucker. Rumour has it that he may have been a 'drugs baron'. However, this cannot be substantiated. He was more likely to have been running his father's patent medicine business.

About 1910, he moved into a newly built house at 149 Half Moon Lane, at the corner with Elmwood Road. Some of the boundary walls survive and the number '149' is still visible on the Elmwood Road entrance brick pier.

A stone plaque inscribed 'WGT's WALL', next to 74 Elmwood Road, suggests that Tucker may have had disputes with his neighbours.

***Walter Tucker's Plaque***

In 1912 his wife Helen Adelaide (née Pickett) died there aged 33. About 1925 he moved away, probably returning to the USA. He died on 7 April 1958 at Cook, Illinois.

The house was damaged by a landmine in 1940 and was demolished in the 1950s. The site is now flats built by Southwark Council, 76-106 Elmwood Road.

## Sir Henry Tulse (d 1689)
## Landowner & Lord Mayor of London

Sir Henry Tulse, businessman, politician and landowner, gave his name to Tulse Hill. His origins are obscure. After the English Civil War, he is known to have owned around 250 acres of land in the Herne Hill area, some of which were later to become part of Brockwell Park.

Sir Henry's family came from Hampshire; and from 1640 to 1661 he was MP for Christchurch. However, he made his fortune in trade, probably mainly from slavery. He was an Associate of the Royal Africa Company, which in the 1680s was supplying over 5,000 slaves annually to the West Indies. Through his business activities he became very wealthy, owning lands in Hampshire and Surrey as well as what is now Tulse Hill and the surrounding area. He also owned several London houses, including two on London Bridge.

Sir Henry was a member and office holder of a number of City institutions and a Lieutenant of the City of London. He was knighted in 1673 and became an Alderman in the same year, a position he held for 16 years. He was also highly regarded for his philanthropy. There was, however, a short gap in his Aldermanic reign when he was temporarily displaced by James

***Henry Tulse Shield***

II because of a dispute over the role of the established church. In 1683-84 he was Lord Mayor of London.

Sir Henry and his wife Elizabeth had at least two children, Jane Elizabeth and a son also called Henry. His daughter married Richard, the first Lord Onslow (1654-1717) and Speaker of the House of Commons. In November 1718 Jane Elizabeth committed suicide by drowning herself in a pond on the Archbishop of Canterbury's estate at Croydon.

Sir Henry died 30 August 1689. In his will he asked to be buried in the parish church of St Thomas Bartholomew, London; but there is no record of his wish being carried out.

## Sir William Vestey (1859-1940)
## 165 Denmark Hill
## Businessman and Trader

One of six sons of a provision merchant, William Vestey was born in Liverpool. Together with his brother Edmund he gained experience in the family business; he was sent, aged 17, to the USA to buy and ship home goods for his father. William established a canning factory in Chicago, making corned beef from the cheaper cuts of meat, and shipped them to Liverpool.

Deciding to exploit the use of refrigeration to preserve foodstuffs, the brothers helped establish the first cold store in Liverpool. Their Cold Union Storage Company was to become one of the world's largest such operations, with a world-wide supply network for perishable foods.

The Vesteys were the first to import beef from South America in refrigerated ships. They began by buying two steamers, converting them into refrigeration ships and founding the Blue Star Line (registered 1911). The Vestey empire grew and they acquired the largest refrigerated fleet in the world, 2,365 retail butchers shops in the UK and small freezing works in Australia and New Zealand.

Their cattle-raising farms and ranches gave the Vesteys control of Argentinean supplies to their meat-packing and cold storage plants. However, after Britain's 1914 Finance Act was passed, high taxes made the Vesteys tax exiles and they based their operations in Argentina.

William and his brother returned to England in 1919. They devised a complex and highly successful scheme which avoided them paying any personal tax. This showed them to be as innovative and pioneering in the field of tax avoidance as in the food business.

William Vestey was created a baronet in 1913 for his role in making cheap food more widely available. During WW1, Sir William leased his home, Bessemer House, 165 Denmark Hill (purchased 1910), to the War Office for use as a hospital for convalescing soldiers. Lady Vestey volunteered her help in another property in temporary use as a soldiers' convalescent home - Kingswood House in Dulwich. She so admired Kingswood House that in 1919 Sir William bought the estate. In 1922 he was created Baron Vestey of Kingswood, having bought his title, it was said, for £25,000 from the Lloyd George government. The peerage provoked a letter of protest from King George V, who felt it wrong that a man who declined to pay national taxes should be ennobled.

Sir William Vestey was married twice: first to Sarah Ellis (d 1923), then in New York to Evelene Brodstone (1875-1941). Evelene had joined the Vesteys' Chicago organisation as a secretary in 1895 and became a powerful figure in the business as its international trouble-shooter.

Sir William was a generous host. He frequently entertained and made the grounds of Kingswood House available to many local children. Bomb damage during WW2 made it necessary for the Vesteys to move to another house, in Gerrards Cross. Sir William died there 10 December 1940; his ashes are interred in the Anglican Cathedral, Liverpool. By the time of William's death, the multinational Vestey Corporation was conservatively valued at over £90 million.

## Thomas Vyse (1782-1861)
## The Abbey, 70 Herne Hill
## Straw Hat Manufacturer

In 1805, Thomas Vyse started business as a straw hat manufacturer at 76 Holborn Bridge in London, making superior quality hats. Luton and Dunstable were the main centres for straw plait, but Luton bonnets were of a less good quality and there was little demand in London. However, after the Napoleonic Wars, London hatters extended their manufacturing operations to Luton and Dunstable, and an explosion of trade occurred. Vyse opened his Luton factory in 1826, employing 500 workers in the sewing rooms. Branches were later opened in Tuscany, Paris and New York. By 1850, Vyse's London operations had moved to Wood Street in the City, an area noted at this time for its drapers, milliners and haberdashers. Vyse and Sons became a limited company in 1900 and survived until 1961.

Thomas Vyse was born in Warwickshire, the fifth son of a Birmingham merchant, Andrew Vyse (there is a Vyse Street in the Birmingham Jewellery Quarter). In 1801 he married Alice Crook at Hornsey and moved to The Abbey, 70 Herne Hill in the 1830s. This was located where Herne Hill Mansions now stand. The name 'Abbey' was probably chosen because it may have been built in the Gothic-Revival style resembling a medieval abbey. The grounds extended along the west side of Herne Hill incorporating the present petrol station, Post Office sorting office, Sainsbury's, plus 351-381 Milkwood Road, Abbey Mansions and most of Herne Hill Station.

The whole property was compulsory purchased by the London, Chatham and Dover Railway to build Herne Hill Station, which opened in 1862. The house, with much less land, was sold by auction in 1866. It was given the number 70 in 1883 and demolished in 1898.

Thomas Vyse died 8 January 1861, before the railway was completed. He is interred in the catacombs at Norwood Cemetery.

Vyse's daughter, Maria Louisa, married another straw-hat maker, John Davis Welch (1819-80). They lived, with their three sons and nine daughters, at 39 Herne Hill, a large detached house once situated opposite Gubyon Avenue. The house was renumbered 121 in 1913 and demolished in the 1950s.

## Sir Mortimer Wheeler (1890-1976)
## 16 Rollscourt Avenue
## Archaeologist

Robert Eric Mortimer Wheeler was born in Glasgow to Robert Wheeler, a journalist, and his wife Emily. Soon after Mortimer's birth the family moved: first to Edinburgh, then to Bradford. In 1905 they came to London where his father took over the office of his newspaper, the *Yorkshire Observer*. Their first London home was Carlton Lodge, which is still standing in South Croxted Road near the corner with Park Hall Road. The house proved too small, so in 1908 the family moved to 16 Rollscourt Avenue. Of his new home Mortimer wrote: "We are in a typical semi-detached villa which is, however, most fortunately on the only hill in the district, so that from my window I can see over miles of chimney tops to the two most famous gasworks in England - those of Battersea and Westminster."

In 1907 Mortimer began studies at University College, London, taking an MA (1912) followed by a D.Lit. and winning the first Franks Studentship in Archaeology in 1913.

His first job was with the Royal Commission on Historical Monuments. He rapidly rose through the profession to become one of this country's foremost and best known archaeologists. In 1920 he was appointed Keeper of Archaeology in the National Museum of Wales, and in 1924 was promoted to Director. From 1926 to 1944 he was Director of the London Museum. With the help of his first wife Tessa he founded the University of London's Institute of Archaeology. The Institute was formally established in 1937; but Tessa had died the previous year. It was the largest university-based archaeological institution in Britain. In March 1939 Mortimer married Mavis, the ex-wife of Horace de Vere Cole and former mistress of the artist Augustus John. However, they divorced three years later on the grounds of Mavis' adultery.

Mortimer's archaeological career was interrupted by service in both World Wars; he served as an artillery officer, rising to the rank of Brigadier in WW2. After working in India as Director-General of Archaeology, and as archaeological adviser to the new state of Pakistan, in 1948 he returned to Britain as Professor at the Institute of Archaeology, a position he held until 1955.

Mortimer was particularly well known for his innovatory excavations at Verulamium (a former Roman town where St Albans is today) and Maiden Castle (an Iron Age hill fort in Dorset), as well as for his work in India and Pakistan. He wrote a number of popular books on archaeology, and became famous as an early television personality, appearing frequently in three popular programmes: *Animal, Vegetable, Mineral?* (1952-60), *Buried Treasure* (1954-59) and *Chronicle* (1966). In 1954 he was chosen as TV Personality of the Year. He was knighted in 1952 and became a Fellow of the Royal Society in 1968.

Mortimer lived at 16 Rollscourt Avenue from 1908 until 1924. His parents remained there until 1936. He died 22 July 1976 while living in Leatherhead, Surrey.

## Gabriel White (1902-88)
## 88 Holmdene Avenue
## Artist and Art Administrator

Born in Rome on 29 November 1902, Gabriel Ernest Edward Francis White came to England with his parents in 1911. Educated at Downside School and at Trinity College, Oxford, from 1926-29 he studied art under Bernard Meninsky (1891-1950) at Westminster School of Art, and to 1930 under Frederick Porter (1883-1944) at the General School of Arts and Crafts. In 1930 he held his first solo exhibition at the Major Gallery, London. During WW2 he served with the Royal Engineers on camouflage work, reaching the rank of Lieutenant-Colonel.

From 1945-70 Gabriel worked for the Arts Council of Great Britain. Here he excelled as an administrator, first as Assistant Director of Art, and from 1958 as Director of Art. He was involved with the Council's vast art exhibition programme and was able to empathise with the artists, having been one himself. In 1953 he was awarded the Order of the Aztec Eagle, 2nd class, by the Mexican Government for his work on the Mexican exhibition at the Tate Gallery. In the 1960s, when the Hayward Gallery was being built, it was on White's recommendation that natural light be made available in the upper galleries. The Hayward gallery opened in 1968 with three of Gabriel White's exhibitions: Matisse, van Gogh, and frescoes from Florence. On retiring from the Arts Council, he returned to painting, mainly landscapes, and had several solo exhibitions.

It was while a student at Westminster School of Art that Gabriel White met the illustrator Edward Ardizzone (1900-79), who became a lifelong friend. In 1928 he married Ardizzone's sister, Elizabeth (d 1958). In 1963 he married Jane Kingdon, moving to 88 Holmdene Avenue c1965. In 1979 White published a book about his friend, *Edward Ardizzone – Artist and Illustrator*. He died 13 January 1988.

Gabriel White laid claim to having been the last artist to have painted the Crystal Palace from life. He was actually there with his easel on the afternoon of 30 November 1936 when the infamous fire broke out.

## Bransby Williams (1870-1961)
## 57 Rutland Court
## and Flat 1, Abbey Mansions
## Actor

Bransby Williams was born Bransby William Pharez on 14 August 1870 in Hackney, to William, a printer and his wife Margaret. Bransby had a rather modest upbringing, the family having lost a great deal of money in the 1865 collapse of the Overend, Gurney bank. Ill health put paid to early ambitions to become a missionary; so he took a job as a messenger boy with a firm of tea merchants, then as a clerk with a paper manufacturer. He developed an early fascination with the theatre and music hall, gaining experience as an amateur before deciding to turn professional. His speciality was impersonating popular actors, such as Henry Irving and Beerbohm Tree. After early struggles and some years in various touring companies, his big break came on 26 August 1896, after an appearance at the London Music Hall, Shoreditch.

Bransby now began to play at all the leading London and provincial music halls. By 1897 he was so popular that he shared top of the London Pavilion bill with Dan Leno. He later became one of the first variety artists to appear at a royal command performance. Also in 1897 he began to perform the studies of Charles Dickens' characters for which he became particularly well known.

His large repertoire included Scrooge, Mr Micawber, Peggotty, Uriah Heep, Bill Sykes, Fagin and Sydney Carton. Much of the fascination of Bransby Williams' performance lay in the skill with which he dressed for each part, making lightning costume and make-up changes in full view of the audience. Later he added scenes from Shakespeare as well as dramatic monologues and recitations to his act. These included such works as 'How We Saved the Barge', 'The Yogi's Curse' and 'The Green Eye of the Little Yellow God'. His versatility was such that he also undertook many 'straight' roles, as well as playing pantomime dames.

Bransby Williams' long and varied career was not without its problems. In 1921, while appearing at the London Palladium, he broke his contract to be with his wife after she had been injured in a car accident, perhaps the cause of her death. The consequent black-listing, the rapid decline in the popularity of the music hall and an ill-fated overseas theatrical tour reduced him from one of the highest paid performers to near poverty. However, with the coming of television, he bounced back and made many appearances. For a number of years, his television performance as Scrooge was an annual Christmas Eve fixture.

Bransby Williams married his wife Emilie in 1892. The couple had had two sons and three daughters. Their eldest son, Captain W (Sonny) Bransby Williams MC, went missing in action in France on 12 May 1917, while with the Royal Flying Corps. This loss touched Bransby very deeply, affecting him for the rest of his life. Two of his other children, Eric and Winifred, followed Bransby into acting, also with some success (Eric appeared in around 18 films in the 1920s and 1930s). However, they both eventually left the profession - Winifred to marry and Eric to go into business.

Bransby moved house many times throughout his career. He and his family lived at 17 Pembury Road, in Hackney and later 25 Rodenhurst Road, Clapham Park. From 1911-19 they lived at 102 Upper Tulse Hill, and in the 1920s and 1930s in St John's Wood and East Finchley. He also had a house in Selsey Bill. In 1938 he came to live at 57 Rutland Court, Denmark Hill, in a flat in the newly built block at the rear. The actress Kathleen Saintsbury came here to look after him when he became ill. She had played the lead in many of his company's productions, but gave up her own acting career to nurse him. She was to stay with Bransby for the rest of his life.

During the war, Bransby and Kathleen moved to Flat 1, Abbey Mansions, a block of four purpose-built flats dating from around 1900, located behind Herne Hill Mansions and 381 Milkwood Road. The now derelict block is at the end of a short path between the garage and No. 381.

Bransby and Kathleen shared this flat until his death on 3 December 1961, at a nursing home at 38 Palace Road, Streatham.

## George Williams (1910-95)
## 18 Fawnbrake Avenue
## Comedian

George Williams was born in Liverpool 25 May 1910; his farming family moved to Nottingham a few years later. He made his first stage appearance aged four, joined a local concert party at nine singing and doing small sketches, and had his own stage school at 16. His professional debut was at the

Accrington Hippodrome. In WW2 he entered the National Fire Service and joined ENSA, doing nearly 3,000 shows for British and American troops.

In July 1944 he opened at the Shepherd's Bush Empire and soon became a top-of-the-bill comic on the Moss Empire circuit of variety theatres with such stars as Jessie Matthews and Gracie Fields. He also broadcast regularly on BBC radio shows such as *Midday Music Hall*, *Workers' Playtime* and *Variety Bandbox*, alternating with Frankie Howerd. He toured with Macari's Dutch Serenaders for three years in *Dutch Mill* and every Christmas was in demand as pantomime Dame, Buttons or Simple Simon. His first TV shows were *Lucky Dip* and *Way Out West* from Alexandra Palace, where he later returned for live appearances in Horace Mashford's *Palace of Varieties*.

On stage, looking gaunt in crumpled clothes, cloth cap and chalk-white face make-up, he delighted audiences with his catch-phrase, "I'm not well." With perfect timing, he would expand, in broad Lancashire accent, "...in fact, I'm... proper poorly!" A classic camp comic, he always presented effeminate characters, such as the limp-wristed soldier mistakenly recruited despite being medically unfit.

Then during the 1952/53 pantomime season at the Kemble Theatre, Hereford, Williams was arrested for homosexual offences involving National Servicemen from Bryanston Army Camp. He served 18 months of a two-year sentence. Dropped by Moss Empire and the BBC, his career was effectively over.

In 1967 Williams moved to 18 Fawnbrake Avenue, a shared house, where he lived the rest of his life. With

homosexual acts between consenting adults decriminalised and more liberal attitudes generally, Williams at last made a comeback. Appearing at such venues as 'The Establishment', he was discovered by a younger generation. During the 1970s he was a popular guest star at variety entertainment venues and appeared in *Joseph and the Amazing Technicolor Dreamcoat*. Booked for a fortnight at the Players Theatre, he stayed 14 weeks; and in 1985 he received a standing ovation at the London Palladium as special guest of the British Music Hall Society (BMHS). Keen to help young artistes, he assisted impresario Alexander Bridge in many BMHS shows.

Williams also painted portraits of famous stars, giving exhibitions in theatres and the Ideal Homes Show. A tireless worker for charity, he aided the Variety Artistes Ladies Guild and helped at the Stars' Bazaar for half a century. A devout Quaker, he regularly attended at Streatham Friends and Westminster Meeting House.

In 1990 he was made life President of the Derbyshire and Nottingham Music Hall Society. In 1992, with the encouragement of his friend Millicent Freshfield, he completed his autobiography, *Hang on a Tick*. The great Marcel Marceau, to whom Williams had dedicated his poem 'I Name Thee Clown', wrote an introduction, describing Williams as "Britain's most underrated comedian." An 'agent' offered to publish the book. However, having taken the £15 subscriptions, he used the money to cross-subsidise other projects and then disappeared.

George Williams died 23 April 1995. That September, colleagues, friends and admirers attended a memorial service at St Paul's Covent Garden, featuring his writings and songs.

## James Wilson (1760-1814)
## 170 Denmark Hill
## Sea Captain and Trader

James Wilson led an exciting seafaring life, full of stirring adventures. Born in Newcastle-on-Tyne, he was the youngest son of 19 children. His father, a Merchant captain, brought him up to be familiar with life on board ship. During the American War of Independence James was present at the battles of Bunker Hill (1775) and Long Island (1776).

In about 1780, James Wilson sailed to Calcutta as mate on an East Indiaman. There he joined the local Indian transport ships, carrying supplies to the British Forces. This was dangerous work since France and Britain were at war over the control of India. In 1781, the Governor of Madras provided Wilson with four ships and orders to take supplies to the British troops near Cuddalore under the command of Sir Eyre Coote (1726-83). These troops were surrounded by the forces of Hyder Ali (c1722-83), the Muslim ally of the French. The sea route had been cut off by French warships anchored at Pondicherry. However, Wilson successfully ran the French blockade and delivered the supplies.

After this skirmish, Wilson continued to carry material for the military, but was eventually captured by the French who then sold him and many other prisoners to Hyder Ali for 300,000 rupees. Wilson managed a bold escape by jumping 40 feet into the alligator-infested River Coleroon. He covered a distance of 40 miles, some by canoe, before being re-captured. Wilson and his fellow prisoners were then forced to march 500 miles, before being imprisoned for 22 months in the infamous Black Hole of Seringapatum. Out of an initial 153 occupants, he was one of only 32 who survived.

On his release and after a period of convalescence, Wilson resumed trading in India. By 1793 he had made enough money to retire, returning to England and settling in Horndean, Hampshire. He became a member of the Orange Street Chapel in Portsea, and influenced by the sermons and private instruction of the pastor, Rev. John Griffin, became an ardent Christian. Introduced to the newly formed London Missionary Society, he was persuaded to lead their first enterprise, a voyage to the South Pacific Islands with 30 missionaries on board. From his own pocket Wilson bought the ship *Duff*. From 1796-98 he captained the ship visiting Otaheite, the Friendly and Sandwich Islands and the Marquesas.

On his return, Wilson, by then aged 38, married Elizabeth Holbert and settled at 170 Denmark Hill, next door to Samuel Sanders. They had one son and three daughters.

From 1806 Wilson served as a deacon of York Street Chapel (see George Clayton), where his father-in-law, Richard Holbert, had been a founder member. Wilson died 12 August 1814 and was buried at the Chapel. His tomb still remains in Browning Street, although the chapel was destroyed by fire in 1979.

When Ruskin Park was being laid out in 1906-07, it was decided to retain the portico and wall of Wilson's former house to create a shelter, now a well-known wisteria-covered feature in the park. Wilson had served as a director of the London Missionary Society from 1798-1814. Soon after Ruskin Park opened in 1907, the Society placed a commemorative plaque to him (unfortunately now disappeared) on the portico.

## Prof. Alan Waller Woodruff (1916-92)
## 122 Ferndene Road
## Physician

Alan Waller Woodruff was born 27 June 1916. He studied medicine and surgery at Durham University and worked as a surgeon at Newcastle upon Tyne Royal Infirmary. He moved to London in 1948 to take a Senior Lectureship at the London School of Hygiene and Tropical Medicine; and for the rest of his career he specialised in tropical medicine.

Alan held posts at a number of London hospitals, including the Wellcome Professor of Clinical Tropical Medicine at the London School of Hygiene and Tropical Medicine, and consultancies to the army, British Airways and the World Health Organisation. He was also Professor of Medicine at the University of Juba, Sudan and a Visiting Professor at universities in Egypt, Iraq and Libya.

In 1946, Alan married Mercia Arnold. They had a son, also called Alan, and a daughter, Heather. The family moved to 122 Ferndene Road in 1982 and were still living there when Alan died on 12 October 1992.

***London School of Hygiene and Tropical Medicine***

## Charles Woolley (1846-1922)
## 35 Dulwich Road
## Businessman and Alderman

Charles Woolley was born in Clapham 30 November 1846, the son of Nathaniel Woolley, a doctor, of Ecton, Northamptonshire. Educated privately and at King's College, London, he was in his youth an accomplished sportsman.

Charles married Elizabeth Bone; the couple lived at 19 Haycroft Road, Brixton and had a son and two daughters. From 1890-1910 he was Secretary of the National Discount Company. He was also Director of Consolidated Electrical Co Ltd and Anglo-Portuguese Telephone Co Ltd, and Fellow of the Incorporated Society of Accountants and Auditors, Institute of Bankers, Charted Institute of Secretaries (also President), Chartered Institute of Directors and Royal Geographical Society. He gave expert evidence before a House of Lords Select Committee on amendments to Lord Dudley's Bill on company law reform, which came into effect in January 1901.

Elected Conservative Councillor for Tulse Hill Ward (which then included Poet's Corner, Herne Hill) in the newly formed Metropolitan Borough of Lambeth, he served from 1900-12, chairing the Finance, Lighting and Watch Committees. In 1905 the Woolleys moved to 35 Dulwich Road, on the corner with Shakespeare Road. Charles named the house Verulam after St Albans, where his grandfather had been Mayor. He became an Alderman in 1906.

He was a churchwarden of St Mary Lambeth, devoting himself to charitable and educational work. As an

***Doulton Vase from the Woolley Collection***

inventor, he was patentee of pneumatic tyres for cycles and vehicles. A member of the London Press Club and Chartered Institute of Journalists, he published books on finance and travels, contributed press and magazine articles on Lambeth and wrote fiction.

With his antiquarian interests, he collected books, coins and stoneware. In April 1915 he presented over 200 items of pottery, including 54 Doulton pieces, to Lambeth, plus a large number of prints and topographical photographs. His objective was to form the nucleus for a Borough Museum. When in 1922 the Wellcome Laboratories were leaving Brockwell House, Woolley wrote urging the Council to seek permission from the LCC to use the house for a Museum of Lambeth. A week later, on 5 August 1922, Charles Woolley died of a heart attack; he is buried in Norwood Cemetery. Despite Lambeth's pleas, Brockwell House was demolished. The Woolley Collection, legacy of the 'Historian of Lambeth', rests with Lambeth Archives at the Minet Library and may be viewed by appointment.

## William Bessemer Wright (1858-1940) 167 Denmark Hill Porcelain Collector

William Bessemer Wright was the son of William Wright (1827-1908), chief clerk at Trinity House, and Elizabeth Bessemer (1827-1915). They lived at The Grange, 167 Denmark Hill. This was a house built for them in 1865 by his grandfather, the inventor Sir Henry Bessemer, who lived next door. The Grange, demolished in 1947, was located near Tayside Court, Basingdon Way. William Bessemer Wright lived there until 1885 when he married Alice Armstrong (1860-1957) and moved to Hillside, 1 Champion Hill. Ruskin Park House flats now occupy the site. About 1895 he moved to Kensington, moving again in 1920 to Batchworth Heath House near Rickmansworth, where he died 7 July 1940.

Bessemer Wright formed a successful partnership with William Ford in the firm of Ford and Wright, diamond merchants, cutters and polishers. Sir Henry Bessemer wrote in his autobiography that "in the year 1884...I was...engaged designing the whole of the machinery about to be erected by my grandson, William Bessemer Wright, at the new diamond mills in Clerkenwell." In 1894 the firm became Ford and Co; it ceased business c1902.

Bessemer Wright was an enthusiastic billiard player, and in 1921 was elected to the Billiards Association and Control Council. He was also a passionate collector of porcelain, the bulk of his collection being formed by the mid-1920s.

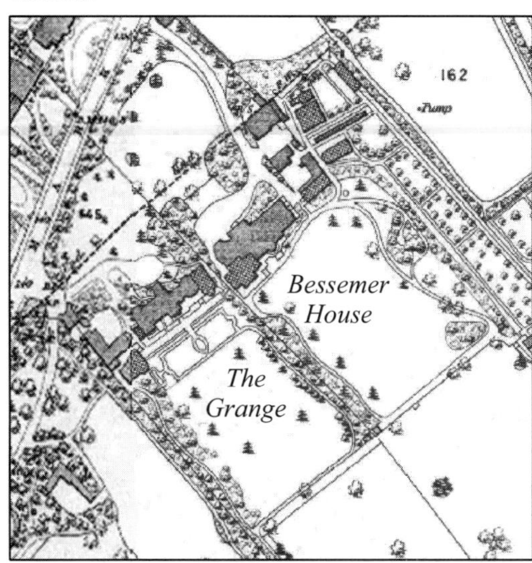


***Map of The Grange and Bessemer House in Denmark Hill c1870***

His grand-daughter, Mrs Adam Smith, née Felicity Bessemer Semon (1914-89) bequeathed to the National Trust the collection of fine 18th century English porcelain, known as the Bessemer Wright Collection. Of the original 200 pieces, 81 are displayed at Mompesson House, Salisbury. A few pieces were sold and the remainder distributed among four other National Trust properties (Attingham, Kedleston, Ormsby Hall and Osterley).

## Edward Yates (1838-1907)
## 56 Half Moon Lane
## Speculative Builder

Born in Shrewsbury, Edward Yates came to London in the 1850s to seek his fortune, starting work as a builder's labourer. In the 1861 census he is described as a bricklayer, living at 9 Henry Street, Lambeth. The street is now called Oval Way, off Kennington Lane. In the 1871 census, he is shown as a builder living at 2 York Street, London Road, Southwark, in one of his own houses adjoining his office. York Street later became Skipton Street; the Elephant and Castle Bakerloo Underground Station now occupies the site.

Using a building society loan and taking advantage of an upswing in the market, in 1867 Yates built twelve houses, for sale or lease, at Nine Elms. Through an agreement with an established local builder, Henry Nixon, he found the prospective house buyers. The profit from the sales was to help fund the next scheme.

In 1868 Yates built 46 terraced houses at Dragon Road, off St George's Way in North Peckham. These were predominantly for letting rather than for sale, a gamble that paid off. He borrowed about £7,000 at 5% for 14 years. On each house he spent £190 and received £26 yearly in rent. His profit was small; however, it enabled him to continue building and later to prosper, even during times of recession, by relying on the regular income from rents.

At first Yates concentrated on projects in Walworth and Camberwell. He thus ensured that each tenant was within walking distance of the estate's office, to make it easier to pay the rent. He also went into a limited partnership with a local builder, S Sansom of Kennington. This helped ensure continuity of work and economies in building costs. The partnership lasted 17 years. Among the streets he developed were Aldbridge, Chatham, Darwin, Flinton, Larcom, Princess and Villa Streets, Domville Grove and part of Surrey Square - many have since disappeared. His largest project, begun in 1877, was the Waverley Park estate, to the south and east of Nunhead Cemetery. It mainly encompassed Ivydale, Limesford and Athenlay Roads, and was destined to be one of the largest such developments in South London.

In 1885 Yates moved his office to 194 Walworth Road; today (2006) there is still a Yates Estate office at 205 Walworth Road. By 1905 he owned 2,345 houses, nearly one third in Nunhead.

He married Mary Ann in 1859 and they had five daughters and one son. They lived for a time at 41 Kennington Park Road, moving c1890 to Ivyhurst, (later No. 56) Half Moon Lane, where he remained until his death. Yates died 26 April 1907 at Shore Hall, Finchingfield, Essex; he is buried in Norwood Cemetery. He left £921,432 in his will.

# SOURCES

## BOOKS:

Ackerley, Joe *My Father and Myself* (1968)

Aldrich, Megan ed. *The Craces: Royal Decorators 1768-1899* (1990)

Barnes, George Nicoll *From Workshop to War Cabinet* (1924)

Batchelor, John *John Ruskin, No Wealth but Life* (2000)

Bergh, Tony van den *Who Killed Freddie Mills?* (1991)

Bessemer, Sir Henry *Sir Henry Bessemer FRS* (1989)

Bicknell, Algernon ed. *Hafiz of Shiraz: selections from his poems, translated from the Persian by Herman Bicknell* (1875)

Bicknell, Algernon *Five Pedigrees* (1912)

Blanch, W H *The Parish of Camberwell* (1875; reprint 1976)

Bloice, Brian; Gower, Graham and Marchant, Daphne *Park Hill Streatham* (2004)

Boase, Frederic *Modern English Biography*

Boast, Mary *The Story of Camberwell* (1996)

Boast, Mary *The Story of Dulwich* (1990)

Brace, Geoffrey *Anna ... Susanna* (1991)

Bressler, Fenton *Freddie Mills: a puzzle*; published in *Unsolved Murders and Mysteries* ed. John Canning (1987)

British Biographical Index

Buckland, C E *Dictionary of Indian Biography* (1906)

Buckman, David *The Dictionary of Artists in Britain since 1945* (1998)

Burke's Landed Gentry

Calder-Marshall, A *Havelock Ellis a Biography* (1959)

Campbell, Beatrice Stella *My Life and Some Letters* (1922)

Canning, John ed. *Unsolved Murders and Mysteries* (1987)

Chambers Biographical Dictionary

Church, Richard *Over the Bridge* (1955)

Church, Richard *The Golden Sovereign* (1957)

Cleal, Edward E *The Story of Congregationalism in Surrey* (1908)

Cook, E T and Wedderburn, A ed. *The Complete Works of John Ruskin* (1904)

Cook, E T *Home and Haunts of John Ruskin* (1912)

Cowley, Richard *Policing Northamptonshire 1836 -1986* (1986)

Crockford's Clerical Directory

Darby, Patrick *Kingswood, A History of the House and Estate* (1999)
Davies, Hunter *A Walk Around the Lakes* (1979)
Dawson-Scott C A *From Four Who are Dead* (1926)
Dearden, J S *John Ruskin, An Illustrated Life 1819-1900* (1981)
Dearden, J S *John Ruskin's Camberwell* (1990)
Dearden, J S ed. *The Professor: A Severn's memoir of John Ruskin* (1967)
Debrett's Peerage and Baronetage
Dictionary of Business Biography
Dictionary of National Biography
Donati, William *Ida Lupino, a Biography* (1996)
Draper, Marie P G *Lambeth Open Spaces, An Historical Account* (1979)
Dyos, H J *Exploring the Urban Past: Essays in Urban History* (1982)
Dyos, H J *Victorian Suburb: A study of the growth of Camberwell* (1961)
Edwards, Rhoda *Lambeth Stoneware* (1973)
Ernest, Johanna *The Life of Dorothy Kerrin* (1983)
Evans, Joan *John Ruskin* (1954)
Fani-Kayode, Rotimi *Black Male / White Male* (1988)
Felstead, S T *Sir Richard Muir, a memoir of a public prosecutor* (1927)
Flanagan, Bob *West Norwood Cemetery's Sportsmen* (1995)
Fox, M R *Dye-Makers of Great Britain 1856-1976* (1987)
Friends of Ruskin Park *A Mini-Guide to Ruskin Park* (2002)
Fullerton, W Y *The Church Under the Hill - Denmark Place, Camberwell* (c1923)
Gladwyn, Derek *Leigh Park, a 19th century pleasure park* (1992)
Green, Brian *Dulwich, a history* (2002)
Greeves, Lydia and Trinick, Michael *The National Trust Guide* (1996)
Grimshaw, Anna ed. *The C L R James Reader* (1992)
Grosskurth, P *Havelock Ellis - A Biography* (1980)
Grove Dictionary of Art
Grove's Dictionary of Music and Musicians
Halley, Ned *Sandeman: Two Hundred Years of Port and Sherry* (1990)
Hawkes, Jacquetta *Mortimer Wheeler – Adventurer in Archaeology* (1982)
Herne Hill Society *Herne Hill Heritage Trail* (2003)
Hilton, Tim *John Ruskin, the Early Years* (1985)
Hirst, Alex *The Last Supper: a Creative Farewell to Rotimi Fani-Kayode* (1992)
International Directory of Films and Film Makers
James, C L R *Beyond a Boundary* (1963)
Jenkyns, Patricia *The Book of Herne Hill* (2004)

Jenkyns, Patricia *The Story of Sir Henry Bessemer* (1984)

Jones, Reginald V *Most Secret War British Scientific Intelligence 1939-45* (1978)

Kelly's Post Office London Directories

Kilgarriff, Michael *Grace, Beauty and Banjos* (1998)

Leon, Derrick *Ruskin the Great Victorian* (1949)

Lockett, Richard *Samuel Prout* (1985)

London County Council *Names of Streets and Places in the Administrative County of London* (1929 and 1955)

Lowry, H D *A Dream of Daffodils* (1912)

Lupino, Stanley *From the Stocks to the Stars: an unconventional autobiography* (1934)

Lutyens, Mary *Effie in Venice* (1965)

Lutyens, Mary *Millais and the Ruskins* (1967)

Maddocks, Morris *The Vision of Dorothy Kerin* (1991)

Mann, William J *Behind the Screen* (2001)

Merrifield, Ralph *The Archaeology of Ritual and Magic* (1987)

Morrissey, Kim *Mrs Ruskin* (2003)

Mould, Richard W *Southwark Men of Mark* (1903)

Murphy, Gregory *The Countess* (c2000)

Nichols, Roger *Mendelssohn Remembered* (1997)

Noonan, Damien *The Daily Telegraph Guide to Britain's Historic Houses* (2004)

Normanton, Helena *The Trial of Arthur Rouse* (1931)

Nurse, Bernard ed. *Who Was Who in Dulwich* (2002)

Oxford Companion to Literature

Parker, Peter *Ackerley: A life of J R Ackerley* (1989)

Peters, Margot *Mrs Pat* (1984)

Pine, L G *The New Extinct Peerage 1884-1971* (1972)

Quennel, Peter *John Ruskin, the Portrait of a Prophet* (1949)

Read, Benedict *Victorian Sculpture* (1982)

Ruskin, John *Praeterita* (1886)

Scowcroft, Philip L *British Light Music Composers* (1997)

Stead, Herbert E *Captain James Wilson* (c1909)

Survey of London *vol. 22 Bankside* (1950)

Survey of London *vol. 23 St. Mary Lambeth, South Bank & Vauxhall* (1956)

Survey of London *vol. 25 St. George's Fields* (1955)

Survey of London *vol. 26 St. Mary Lambeth, Southern Area* (1956)

Sutherland, Jonathan *Unsolved Victorian Murders* (2002)

Symons, A J A *Lowry H D, A Memoir and a Bibliography* (1925)

Trafalgar House Group *Trollope and Colls, City Builders for 200 Years, 1778-1978* (1978)

Van Ash, C and Sax Rohmer, E *Master of Villainy* (1972)

Venn, J A *Alumni Cantabrigienses, 1752 to 1900* (1954)

Vincent, Adrian *A Companion to Victorian and Edwardian Artists* (1991)

Wheeler, Sir Mortimer *Still Digging* (1955)

Who Was Who

Who's Who of British Members of Parliament

Who's Who in the Theatre (1912-1961)

Williams, Bransby *An Actor's Story* (1909)

Williams, Bransby *Bransby Williams by Himself* (1964)

Williamson, G C *Bryan's Dictionary of Painters and Engravers* (1904)

Wilson, T L *Some Old Houses of Upminster* (1880)

Woollacott, Ron *Nunhead Notables* (2002)

## Other Publications:

Apollo Magazine

*A Timely Gift, Mrs. Adam Smith's porcelain at Mompesson House, Salisbury* by Anthony Du Boulay (April 1993)

Call Boy, the Journal of the British Music Hall Society

*George Williams* by J O Blake (Autumn 1983)

*Obituary - George Williams* (Summer 1995)

Camberwell Society Camberwell Quarterly

*German Camberwell* by Tony Wilson (April 1999)

Collectanae Londiniensia

*The South Metropolitan Cemetery, West Norwood, and its Memorials* by Eric F Smith (LAMAS 1978)

Friends of Nunhead Cemetery Newsletter

*The Govers* by Ron Woollacott (Winter 1986)

Friends of West Norwood Cemetery Newsletters:

*Christopher Pond* by Paul Graham (July 1994)

*Charles Woolley* by Patricia Jenkyns (September 1996)

*Sir Richard Muir* by Paul Graham (January 1998)

*John Francis Crook* by Bob Flanagan (September 2002)

*Joseph Bernard Clark* by Ellen Barbet (September 2002)

*Frederick James Barthorpe* by John W Brown (September 2003)

*Sydney Bertram Carter* by Bob Flanagan (September 2004)

Furniture History Society Journal

*Luke Lightfoot* by Lindsay Boynton (Volume II 1966)

Herne Hill Society Newsletters:

*Railton Road Methodist Church* (November 1984)

*Charles Woolley* by Patricia Jenkyns (January 1991)

*Reminiscences of Big Ray* (Autumn 2005)

London Topographical Society Newsletter

*William Strudwick* by David Webb (November 2001)

Turner Studies, His Art and Epoch 1775-1851

*The Turner Collector: Elhanan Bicknell*, by Peter Bicknell (1987)

Virginia Quarterly Review

*Effie in Venice and the Roman Spring of Margaret Fuller* by Helen Barolini (Autumn 2002)

# People in this book who are buried in Norwood Cemetery

| Name | Date of burial |
|---|---|
| Alcock, Charles | 2 March 1907 |
| Attwood, Matthias | 18 November 1851 |
| Attwood, Matthias Wolverley | 23 September 1865 |
| Baily, Charles | 7 October 1878 |
| Barthorpe, Sir Frederick | 5 March 1942 |
| Belcher, John | 13 November 1913 |
| Benecke, Mrs Henriette | 31 January 1893 |
| Bessemer, Sir Henry | 19 March 1898 |
| Bicknell, Elhanen | 3 December 1861 |
| Bicknell, Henry Sanford | 1 December 1880 |
| Bird, Frederick | 7 February 1929 |
| Blackburn, Joshua | 24 December 1888 |
| Blackburn, Joshua John Blades | 28 November 1898 |
| Bristowe, Thomas Lynn | 10 June 1892 |
| Chadwick, David | 23 September 1895 |
| Clark, Joe | 5 February 1940 |
| Clements, Fr. Peter | 24 August 1999 |
| Crace, John Diblee | 22 November 1919 |
| Crace, John Gregory | 17 August 1889 |
| Crook, John | 15 November 1922 |
| Culverwell, Robert James | 15 December 1852 |
| Druce, Charles | 5 January 1881 |
| Druce, George | 20 April 1869 |
| Fall, Richard Whiteman | 22 March 1878 |
| Fosbery, James | 9 July 1884 |
| Graham, Christopher | 15 March 1847 |
| Gurney, Joseph | 15 August 1879 |
| Gurney, William Brodie | 31 March 1855 |
| Hunte, Joe | 14 October 1983 |
| Key, Sir John | 20 July 1858 |

Key, Sir Kingsmill Grove .......... 3 January 1900
Leaf, William .......... 9 July 1874
Locke, John .......... 4 February 1880
Lomas, Sophie Crawford .......... 20 April 1929
Longsdon, Alfred .......... 1 December 1893
Lowry, Henry Dawson .......... 25 October 1906
Muir, Sir Richard .......... 16 January 1924
Pigeon, Richard Hotham .......... 18 June 1851
Pond, Christopher .......... 5 August 1881
Prout, Samuel .......... 17 February 1852
Rule, Arthur .......... 9 June 1915
Stone, William .......... 25 August 1857
Tucker, Augustus Quackenbush .......... 12 January 1916
Vyse, Thomas .......... 16 January 1861
Woolley, Charles .......... 11 August 1922
Yates, Edward .......... 3 May 1907

# INDEX

The following conventions should be noted in using this index:

- names of personalities who have entries in the main text are not listed, except where they appear in another entry;
- organizations, firms etc. whose titles start with the same name as that of the personality with whom they are associated (e.g. Ruskin Foundation, Clark & Fenn Ltd) are similarly not listed, as the reference to them may be found in the relevant entry;
- an asterisk after a house name or number indicates a building that has been demolished (in many cases a more recent building has replaced it);
- where the house numbering has been changed, the number given is that which applied at the time when the person associated with it was alive. In most cases the current house number is not given for the sake of brevity (and of the indexer's sanity).

# The Herne Hill Society

Founded in 1982, the Herne Hill Society is a registered charity working to enhance and maintain the quality of the amenities, facilities and environment of the Herne Hill area for the benefit of residents, visitors and tradespeople. Our aims are to encourage high standards of local planning, architecture, transport and other facilities; to explore the area's geography, history and natural history; and to encourage the preservation, protection, development and improvement of features of historic or public interest.

For more information about the Society, please log on to our website at:

*www.hernehillsociety.org.uk*

or contact us at:

The Herne Hill Society
P O Box 27845
London SE24 9XA

Published with the support of
Heritage Lottery Awards for All

ISBN 1 873520 60 3